HINDUTVA AND VIOLENCE AGAINST WOMEN

HINDUTVA AND VIOLENCE AGAINST WOMEN

BRINDA KARAT

SPEAKING TIGER

SPEAKING TIGER BOOKS LLP
125A, Ground Floor, Shahpur Jat, near Asiad Village,
New Delhi 110049

ISBN: 978-93-5447-811-6
eISBN: 978-93-5447-824-6

10 9 8 7 6 5 4 3 2 1

Typeset in Garamond Premier Pro by SÜRYA, New Delhi
Printed at Chaman Enterprises, New Delhi

This book is for you who resist the bulldozer
of majoritarian injustice

Contents

Introduction 9

1. The Bilkis Bano Case 19
2. Ethnic and Communal Majoritarianism in Manipur 31
3. Communal Majoritarianism in 'Normal Times' 45

Acknowledgements 99
Notes 101

Introduction

On August 15, 2022, a historic day when India celebrated seventy-five years of her independence, the Prime Minister of India, Narendra Modi, in his speech on the occasion made a specific reference to women. He said, 'My brothers and sisters, from this rampart of Red Fort, I also want to share an agony. What I wish to share is that it hurts me to say that we have witnessed a perversion in our day-to-day speaking, behaviour. We have been casually using expletives and cuss words which are abusive and against our women. Can we not pledge to get rid of every behaviour and culture that humiliates and demeans women in our daily life? Women's pride is going to be a huge asset in fulfilling the dreams of the nation. I see this power and therefore I am insistent on it.'[1]

A few hours later, in the prime minister's home state of Gujarat, walking out of the Godhra jail were eleven men, convicted of heinous crimes of gang rape of three women and murder of fourteen, including two children. They had been granted remission from the sentence of life imprisonment on grounds of good behaviour in jail. Photographs of the moment showed them being garlanded, rather like heroes returning from the battlefield. Their case had been examined by the central home ministry led by Amit Shah. In a case such as this, it was clear enough that no one would dare sanction such remission without the explicit permission of the top authorities in the government—the powerful home minister, and the prime minister to whom he reports. In fact, in October 2022, the Gujarat government confirmed this. In an affidavit it filed, the Gujarat government told the Supreme Court that its decision to grant premature release to the eleven men—'as part of the celebration of "Azadi ka Amrit Mahotsav"'—had the approval of the central home ministry.[2]

Here was a prime minister agonized by 'cuss words and expletives'—which, true, are derogatory to women—but who allows the premature release of men convicted for heinous acts of gang rape and murder. A prime minister who asks people to make a pledge 'to get rid of every behaviour and culture that humiliates and demeans women', but does not condemn the sickening felicitation of rapists and killers.

Bilkis Bano was the lone survivor of that incident. Thus, the case is known as the Bilkis Bano case.

We know that injustice in cases of violence against women is not something new. I have been involved in the work of the All India Democratic Women's Association (AIDWA) since its formation in 1981. As political workers and active participants in the struggles waged by women's organizations against violence against women, we have known over the decades, of numerous grave cases of injustice, of cases of the vilest brutality, and that violence against women has been the dark shadow that has followed women in all these years of India's independence. We have heard misogynist and sexist language, demeaning and insulting to women from leaders across the political spectrum. We have fought against the commodification of women's bodies and the promotion of cultures which view women as sex objects. We have fought against cultures that seek to relegate domestic violence and abuse against women as being in the 'private' sphere which cannot be spoken about. We have seen that cases of the most extreme cruelty have been faced by Dalit and Adivasi women, positioned as they are at the trijunction of caste, class and patriarchy. We know from our experience, that the violence and arrogance used as a class/caste weapon against poor women is embedded in structures of the existing unequal economic and social relations.

So, if violence against women, including cases of savagery and brutality, has been a dreadful reality for women in India all these decades, what makes the Bilkis Bano case an illustration of the changes occurring in the systems of prevention of violence, punishment for violence, and rehabilitation for a survivor? What are the causes of special concern?

The question prompts us to look deeper into the processes which made it possible for the killers to get themselves released. The phrase 'nature of the case', used by the authorities while citing reasons for their release, acts like a red alert for women activists. What is in the nature of this case apart from it being one of the most heinous of crimes in recent times? Does it mean that it sets the framework for cases of a similar 'nature'? Is it the nature of the case or the nature of the prevailing political environment, the nature of the serving government, the nature of the agenda of the government which was the determining factor? Instead of considering Bilkis Bano's case in an isolated manner, we need to locate it within this larger context.

This essay is essentially about this larger context. In India, women's movements have differed from the framework of analysis which dominated Western women's movements from the decade of the sixties. In the West the main paradigm for analysis had been the relations between men and women, a narrow understanding of patriarchy wrenched away from its socio-economic, political and cultural moorings. In India, we have, through the experience of our own history and through the freedom struggle, understood women's status including the multiple forms and methods of violence against women within the context of the political, socio-economic, cultural realities, including the caste system. Looking at the issue of violence against women in this broader framework shows us the changing dimensions of violence against women in India today. By change I don't necessarily mean something 'new'—the intensification of existing, negative and sometimes toxic trends which due to a host of factors become the dominant trend, also adds up to change.

These changes are occurring as a result of the dominance gained by right-wing communal and sectarian forces in India's political and social life, leading to the formation of a government led by the Bharatiya Janata Party (BJP) and influenced, if not run, by the Rashtriya Swayamsevak Sangh (RSS). Let us call it a joint venture of the RSS and its political wing, the BJP. India has seen several governments formed by different political parties, often through coalitions, all with their own declared programmes. It is a legitimate goal of a political party to seek to implement its own specific agenda of governance. But in the decade of rule of the present dispensation, we can see a fundamentally altered situation in India, because of the nature of the agenda and programme set by the RSS from its inception in 1925—the agenda of building what they term a 'Hindu Rashtra'.

The preamble of the Constitution of India starts with the words 'We the People of India having solemnly resolved to constitute India into a sovereign, socialist, democratic republic...' It does not say 'we, the people of India who belong to the Hindu religion...' Thus, the very slogan of a Hindu Rashtra and the establishment of 'Hindu supremacy' or 'majoritarianism' militates against the Constitution of India. This majoritarianism is not a reference to a democratic majority won through votes, a principle of parliamentary democratic governance. A parliamentary majority also has space for the rights of a parliamentary minority. The growth of majoritarianism in India is linked to the identity of a religious majority, the religion itself being interpreted by the government and increasingly by the state. This is a permanent majority based on a narrow religious identity which strengthens itself by a constant targeting of other beliefs. Majoritarianism of this kind has gained huge traction because a parliamentary majority is being used for this specific purpose to undermine the values of the Constitution towards the fulfilment of the Hindutva agenda.

This has serious implications for women's equality,

autonomy and a rights-based framework which is intrinsically linked to secular values and to equal democratic rights enshrined in the Constitution. In the last decade we have seen the steady growth of ideologies and practices linked to the Hindutva project which directly affect women. I deliberately use the word Hindutva, not Hindu, because the political and ideological project of Hindutva has little to do with the beliefs of the large majority of those who are followers of the Hindu religion. Indeed, it can be said that the Hindutva project seeks to build an overarching Hindutva identity. This necessarily means the dilution if not the elimination of the diversity within the religion itself, the homogenization of expressions of belief. But that is a topic for a different essay.

Returning to the impact of Hindutva on violence against women, there are two aspects which I believe are the essence of the changes.

The first is the targeting of the minority communities, in particular, the Muslim minority, although atrocities against the Christian community have also increased, especially against Christian Adivasis and Dalits. Women of these communities have been specifically affected directly and indirectly as targets of hatred, contempt and sometimes violence. This anti-minority bigotry, a basic premise of Hindutva, is what I call 'communal majoritarianism'.

The second is the intrinsic nature of the Hindutva project which selectively valorizes tradition and customs linked to their perception of the ideal woman as 'pativrata nari'. The underlying text is the *Manusmriti*. We know that the *Manusmriti* is considered by Hindutva advocates as the 'fundamental law' for Hindus. In the words of the founder of Hindutva, V.D. Savarkar, 'Manusmriti is that scripture which is most worshippable after the Vedas for our Hindu Nation and which from ancient times has become the basis of our culture-customs, thought and practice.' When the Constituent Assembly adopted the Constitution in 1949, it was the RSS mouthpiece which led the opposition to the Constitution on the grounds that 'laws as enunciated in the Manusmriti excite the admiration of the world and elicit spontaneous obedience and conformity but this means nothing to our constitutional pundits'.[3] We could have ignored this position as the thinking of an earlier generation for which present-day RSS need not be held responsible. But no, even today top leaders hold the same views. On arguably the most important day for the Hindu Rashtra agenda, the bhumipujan for the Ram Mandir in Ayodhya on August 5, 2020, the RSS chief, Mohan Bhagwat, quoted a verse from the *Manusmriti* extolling the varnashrama dharma, the system of birth-based inequality: 'From a first-born [i.e. a Brahmin] born in that country, let all men on earth learn their respective duties.'[4]

The *Manusmriti*, as is known, contains verses which are an abomination to human rights and dignity. It gives sanction to the most vile practices of the caste system and specifically makes the subordination of women and Dalits a premise for the legal framework it espouses, with graded punishment and penalties based on caste hierarchies. That the RSS chief in 2020 should choose a quote symbolizing Brahminical superiority is symbolic of the Hindutva ideology. This text and other religious texts are used as the glue for the creation of an overarching Hindutva identity, as I have mentioned earlier. Undoubtedly, when such beliefs and ideas are promoted by the state, by institutions run by the state, introduced as texts in educational syllabi, by leaders, it has a deep impact on social relations and thinking. This is what I call 'Manuvadi majoritarianism'.

It would be entirely mistaken to hold that majoritarianism benefits the majority—in this case, Hindus. On the contrary, in the experience of India, majoritarianism and its Manuvadi roots negatively affect the rights of the majority of people and especially those of women and oppressed communities. A corollary is that anyone daring to criticize these texts or the practices and customs being promoted are labelled as anti-Hindu. In this unconstitutional view, it is Hindus who alone can be nationalist, so a critic of texts like the *Manusmriti* promptly gets branded as anti-nationalist.

There is already a fair amount of literature on the impact of Hindutva-driven policies on women. The subversion of institutions; appointment to important positions of those whose only merit is loyalty to the Hindutva ideology rather than the Constitution; the perceptible ideological alignment of certain sections of the judiciary, undermining the principles of justice—these are some of the important aspects of the Hindutva project which also have a direct bearing on the struggles of justice for women against violence. I do not deal with these issues in this essay. Here, I focus on the issue of violence against women in an increasingly majoritarian India with regard to two aspects. First, majoritarianism as communal majoritarianism with one set of consequences for women, and its twin, Manuvadi majoritarianism with a second set of consequences. Both these aspects are interlinked. I draw out the linkages through the experience of some cases/developments that illustrate these trends, and which hold out the prospect of losing what we have gained in our collective struggle against violence on women.

Violence Against Women and the RSS-BJP 'Eco-system'

'Eco-system' is a favourite phrase of the Sangh Parivar, frequently used to deride the Left. At the release of a Marathi book in Pune titled *World-Weakening Leftist Termites*, Mohan Bhagwat cited an example of 'KG students in schools being asked about their private parts' as an attack of the 'Left eco-system' on Indian culture.[5] His statement was likely prompted by a report a month earlier of a viral video of a teacher in Pune who was teaching her KG students a lesson on 'good touch, bad touch'. For the eco-system of the RSS, a lesson commonly used to empower children against sexual abuse is something evil—part of the Left eco-system.

Let us turn the mirror on the BJP-RSS—and examine its dual eco-system of both communal and Manuvadi majoritarianism, and its impact on women.

In RSS literature or in speeches made by their leaders and others of the Sangh Parivar, the words 'rape' or other forms of 'sexual assault' find mention mainly as part of the political agenda of Hindu Rashtra. It was Hindutva founder and icon Savarkar who saw rape of Muslim women as a political weapon essential to teach Muslim invaders a lesson. To not do so when the occasion permits is not virtuous or chivalrous, but cowardly.[6] In Savarkar's reading of history, it was not any or all conquering groups, regardless of religious affinity, who made the women of the defeated their targets. Rather there was 'molestation of Hindu women' by Muslim invaders and this should have resulted in identical treatment of Muslim women by Hindu rulers, an undertaking he describes as 'punishment of the Muslim feminine class'. Revenge rape is not new in cultures of rape. In India we have seen such dreadful cases particularly in caste-based crimes perpetrated in the name of 'honour'. What is striking is how these ideas get translated into action by followers of Savarkar's ideology in the Sangh Parivar today. This is not so much 'revenge' as manufactured lies demonizing the 'other community' to justify 'punishment of the Muslim feminine class'.

This is part of the eco-system of the communalization of sexual crimes, by which I mean the religious identity of the victim and/or the religious identity of the perpetrator determining the approach of powerful leaders who are 'influencers' of public opinion and also the governments they lead. This creates new rape cultures within a communal framework that ultimately affect the processes of justice for all women. When governments grant impunity to perpetrators of sexual crimes when such criminals belong to the majority community, no woman can be safe. But this is the process underway in India today.

1. The Bilkis Bano Case

The Bilkis Bano case is one where the victims were all Muslim and the perpetrators belong to the majority community, most belonging to the upper castes, Brahmins. In fact, the victims of rapes and murders in the Gujarat communal violence in 2002 were targeted precisely because they were Muslim. These were categorically communal crimes. I have mentioned that the criminals in this horrendous and barbaric case were granted remission by the Gujarat government in August 2022. Public interest litigations were filed by several concerned citizens, including a joint petition by the AIDWA vice president Subhashini Ali. Bilkis herself filed a petition in the Supreme Court a month later, in November 2022, with senior lawyer Shobha Gupta representing her. It took a great deal of courage for Bilkis to come to the Court.

'Two days ago,' she said at the time, 'on August 15, 2022 the trauma of the past twenty years washed over me again...when I heard that the eleven convicted men who devastated my family and my life, and took from me my three-year-old daughter, had walked free, I was bereft of words. I am still numb. Today, I can say only this—how can justice for any woman end like this? I trusted the highest courts in our land. I trusted the system, and I was learning slowly to live with my trauma. The release of these convicts has taken from me my peace and shaken my faith in justice. My sorrow and my wavering faith is not for myself alone but for every woman who is struggling for justice in courts. No one enquired about my safety and well-being, before taking such a big and unjust decision. I appeal to the Gujarat government, please undo this harm. Give me back my right to live without fear and in peace. Please ensure that my family and I are kept safe.'

The Gujarat government ignored this plea for justice. It went all out, helped by the central government's Solicitor General, to defend its indefensible act of releasing the criminals. It was a hard time for Bilkis Bano. It took over a year for the final judgement.

When it finally came, the judgement acted like oxygen to revive faith in a system which seemed to have turned its back on justice. On January 8, 2024, a bench of Justices B.V. Nagarathna and Ujjal Bhuyan, in a historic judgement, overturned the remissions and ordered that the criminals return to prison. The judgement was a scathing indictment of the Gujarat government: 'We hold: (1) Government of State of Gujarat had no competence to entertain the applications for remission or pass orders thereon. (2) This Court's order dated 13.05.2022 obtained by fraud a nullity. All proceedings taken in furtherance of the judgement are also vitiated and a nullity in law.' The criminals' appeal to give them more time to surrender was turned down. They are back in jail where they belong.

In a statement, through her legal counsel, Bilkis Bano said, 'I have wept tears of relief. I smiled for the first time in over a year and half. I have hugged my children. It feels like a stone the size of a mountain has been lifted from my chest, and I can breathe again... This is what justice feels like. I thank the honourable Supreme Court of India for giving me, my children and women everywhere, this vindication and hope in the promise of equal justice for all.'

A judicial intervention rescued justice from being completely bulldozed by government orders. But in its many twists and turns, the Bilkis Bano case represents the shifting sands, the weakening of the institutional foundations of justice in today's India. There is a fragility in the system. It is hard to admit but so much depends on the approach not of the norms of judicial reasoning but, increasingly, on the attitude of this or that judge. The Bilkis Bano case is significant in many ways—which is why I start my section on 'communal majoritarianism' with this case.

When I met her at the Iqbal Relief Camp in Godhra in 2002, Bilkis was a young woman of twenty-one. It was just a week after she was subjected to the most barbaric atrocities on March 3, 2002. I was part of a team from the All India Democratic Women's Association and the Gujarat unit of the Communist Party of India (Marxist), who met survivors in the camps across the state from March 10 to 13. The members of the delegation included Subhashini Ali, Kiran Moghe, Mariam Dhawale, along with Arun Mehta (Secretary, CPI[M], Gujarat Committee) and Mahesh Chand, Iva Mehta, Nalini Jadeja and Yashodabehn.

The delegation's report was detailed and comprehensive,

including several testimonies of women who had faced the most horrific violence. I reproduce the report of our meeting with Bilkis:

> B w/o Y from Randhikpur village (District Dahod) is 21 years old, five months pregnant. We meet her in the camp. Frail, motionless, drained of all expression she tells her story in a monotone as though she is speaking of someone else. Muslim houses in her village were attacked by upper caste people from her own village along with outsiders on March 1. She and several of her family members fled. She names them: my baby girl Saleha, my mother, Halima, my sisters, Mumtaz and Munni, my brothers, Irfan and Aslam, my maternal uncle, Majeed, two of my father's sisters, Sugra and Amina, one of their husbands, Yusuf, Amina's son, and three daughters, Shamim, Mumtaz and Medina and Shamim's son Husain. Shamim, she says was nearing her full term. It was difficult for both of them to run.
>
> At first, they escaped to Chundagi village which was 5–6 km away and took shelter with Bijal Damor, the local MLA. Then they were asked to leave since it was not safe and they walked to Kuajher where they were given shelter in a mosque. Here Shamim was delivered of a baby girl by a midwife but they were asked to leave soon afterwards because mosques were a target of the rampaging mobs. Shamim, barely able to walk, her infant being carried by her sister almost dragged by the others, herself, tired, breathless, her baby girl Saleha, insisting on being carried only by her, they somehow managed to reach village Kudra. Here some Adivasi Naikas took pity on Shamim's condition and kept them in their huts. B remembers: They

> were kind to us. Shamim's clothes were dirty. Even though the Adivasis were poor they gave her something clean to wear. They let us rest, but then again we had to move but they came with us, escorting us to the next village, Chhapadvad. B pauses. A woman next to her puts her arm around her. She continues: We had started moving towards Panivela village. It was a remote and hilly place. Suddenly we heard the sound of a vehicle. A truck came with people from our own village and outsiders too. They had not come to help us. They stopped us and then the madness started. They pulled my baby from my arms and threw her away. I and the other women were taken aside and raped. I was raped by three men. I was screaming. They beat me and then left me for dead. When I regained consciousness I found I was alone. All around me were the dead bodies[,] of my family, my baby girl, the newborn baby. They were covered with stones. I lay there the whole night and most of the next day. I do not know when I was conscious and when unconscious. Later I was found by a police squad from Limkheda police station. I was taken to the hospital and then brought here. In the hospital the doctors said that her medical examination had confirmed rape. She has named the people who killed her family members and those who raped her... Her father and her husband have been traced to another camp at Dahod and her brother, Saeed, is with her in Godhra.

The report also includes additional detail about the area where this horror took place. The report says: 'The area in Randhikpur village where this atrocity occurred is the same area where the VHP and the Bajrang Dal had attacked a whole village in early 1999 because they suspected that the village was sheltering inter-community couples (two Hindu girls and two Muslim boys) who had got married. Three hundred and fifty Muslims at that time had been forced to leave the village and had their property ransacked. There was a vicious campaign against them. A few months later the next target was the Christian community who were attacked in August 1999. It was reported at that time that 5,000 VHP and Bajrang Dal members had attacked Christian houses for ten hours while the police took no action.'

The implication is clear enough—precisely because no action was taken in the earlier instances of communal hatred against minority communities by the Hindutva brigades, the impunity had the effect of emboldening others. At that time too Gujarat had a BJP government led by Keshubhai Patel. If action had been taken against those unleashing violence in 1999, a strong message would have been delivered that communal violence targeting the minorities will be strictly dealt with. In the absence of action, the same area witnessed the horrific violence against Bilkis and her family.

Bilkis was reunited with her husband Yakoob. She delivered a baby girl. In the years that followed, with support from human rights defenders, Bilkis the victim became Bilkis the fighter. Hers was a saga of immense bravery. The court process was painful and difficult. The first judgement took six years. On January 21, 2008, a special Central Bureau of Investigation (CBI) court in Mumbai sentenced eleven men to life imprisonment for gang rape and the murder of fourteen members of Bilkis Bano's family. The accused appealed against the judgement. On May 4, 2017, the Bombay High Court upheld the conviction, dismissing the appeals of the convicts, and also, in a significant step for justice, set aside the acquittals of five police persons and two doctors who had deliberately tampered with the evidence in the case to help the killers. Thus, eighteen people were convicted in the case.

After the Bombay High Court judgement, Bilkis, thanking the High Court for its judgement, when asked whether she was unhappy that the death sentence was withheld, is reported as saying, 'I want justice, not revenge. I want my daughters to grow up in a safe India.' She described how for all these years she had lived as a nomad, shifting homes 20–25 times out of fear, mainly because the convicts were frequently allowed out on parole. She said, '[E]ach time they were out on parole, they held meetings and threatened us. We had no hope from the police who were complicit in the crime. I am happy that the high court has punished the accused policemen too.'[7]

But five years later, on August 15, 2022, the very day when India was celebrating the 75th anniversary of its independence, the gates of the Godhra jail were opened and all the eleven men convicted of gang rape and murder of Bilkis Bano's family were released—their term of life imprisonment condoned. They had supposedly been in jail for fourteen years, but jail records show that ten of the eleven men had spent almost three years—more than 1,000 days—out on parole on various pretexts.[8] The eleventh had been on parole for 998 days. Thus, even before their release, the jail authorities in Gujarat had shown their sympathy towards those who had committed the horrific crime. The Supreme Court in one of its comments described the parole 'as the privilege of some convicts'.

Gujarat Additional Chief Secretary (Home) Raj Kumar said that the government considered their remission application as the convicts had served fourteen years in jail as well as due to other factors such as 'age, nature of the crime, [and] behaviour in prison'.

It needs to be said that if the nature of this crime is not enough to lock up anyone for life, then why have this punishment at all! It is not the nature of the crime but the nature of the government and the party that rules it which was the factor. Of the ten members of the panel set up to look into their release, five were office bearers in the BJP. Two of them were BJP MLAs. The decision by the Gujarat government was also against the opinion of the Mumbai trial court that had sentenced them to life imprisonment for rape and murder. The trial court had given a 'negative opinion' on the remission plea, according to a member of the jail advisory committee. Their final release from jail was made possible because of the specific permission given for their release by the home ministry under Amit Shah, one of the most powerful members of the central government headed by Mr Modi. In its affidavit to the Supreme Court, in response to petitions opposing the release of these men, the Gujarat government stated that since the case was investigated by a central agency, it had submitted its recommendation to the centre which 'conveyed the concurrency/approval of the Central Government—for premature release of eleven prisoners, vide its letter dated 11-7-2022'.[9]

But what we see is not just impunity but glorification of those who have committed violence against women.

The leaders of the Vishwa Hindu Parishad arranged a reception where the rapists and killers were garlanded. The MLA, Chandrasinh Raulji, who had been a member of the committee which decided the remission, defended the decision saying, 'They [the criminals] were Brahmins and Brahmins are known to have good sanskaar. It might have been someone's ill intention to corner and punish them.'[10] An obnoxious statement that so clearly reveals the Manuvadi underbelly of rank communalism—a defence of the upper castes who can do no wrong! This man was again given the BJP ticket and won the polls, re-elected as MLA in the state assembly elections of 2022.

Some Issues to Consider

The Death Sentence and Collective Conscience

Around the same time that Bilkis was in the courts fighting for justice, a young woman in the capital, who came to be known as Nirbhaya (fearless) was brutally killed. In this tragic and horrific case, the young woman, the same age as Bilkis when she experienced her trauma, was gang raped, her body brutalized. She succumbed to the grievous injuries sustained during the crime. The perpetrators were a gang of six, one of them a minor. This was in December 2012. In six months, the accused were found guilty and sentenced to death. The final appeal by the convicts was rejected by the Supreme Court and on March 20, 2020, eight years after they had committed the crime, four were hanged to death, one had committed suicide while in jail, and the minor served a three-year term under the juvenile justice laws.

In India, the death sentence is on the statute books and has been upheld in the 'rarest of rare' cases. The Nirbhaya case, in the court's view, qualified for this category, which indeed it did. But the Bilkis case, no less brutal, did not figure in this category. Why? Is it because of the religious identity of the victim and the perpetrators? Nirbhaya was a Hindu upper-caste girl, the criminals were men mainly from the lower castes, from poor families. Bilkis is a Muslim and the perpetrators are all upper-caste Hindus. The use of women's bodies as the site to commit unspeakable sexual crimes during communal violence has never been considered by the courts as among the 'rarest of rare' cases. There has never been a sentence of death in a communally motivated sexual crime and murder of a woman. Why do courts not consider this as the 'rarest of the rare'? Is it because such crimes have become 'normalized'? And because many women were subjected to horrific violence rather than a single woman? How many cases involving a woman or girl belonging to a minority community or an oppressed caste—a Dalit or an Adivasi woman—have passed muster for the 'rarest of rare' classification?

I am against the death sentence precisely because it is so arbitrary and subjective. It is also irreversible if later evidence shows the accused may have been innocent. I support life imprisonment in such cases, which is interpreted by the Supreme Court as 'confinement for the balance of the convict's natural life'. In such cases no remission should be available. With the courts not free from majoritarian bias, the death penalty can also become a dangerous weapon in the communalization of sexual crimes.

There is another disturbing aspect to this. In the Nirbhaya case, the court referred to the crime as 'bound to shock the collective conscience which knows not what to do' and a punishment lesser than death 'would shake the confidence of the public in the judicial system'. This reference to the 'collective conscience' is not new and has been used earlier too in cases where stringent punishment has been given admitting that the expression of public opinion, in favour or against, has influenced the court. Such references go against warnings by other benches against the judiciary turning itself into 'oracles or spokesmen of public opinion'.[11] In a political system where the 'collective conscience' can be manipulated into a majoritarian framework, such reasoning can lead to grave injustice. Conversely, if the 'collective conscience' is subdued or absent, influenced by the identity of the victim or the accused, will the punishment be less? These disturbing questions acquire relevance in today's political scenario.

Accountability of Governments in Justice for Women

A year earlier, the Supreme Court had absolved the then chief minister, Narendra Modi, and his government of any complicity in the genocide in Gujarat. The judgement was a big setback for the principle of accountability in governance. It meant that violence could consume a state for days, there could be killing and rape, burning and looting of houses; in case after case, there could be evidence that the police often were not just spectators but sometimes openly encouraged the mob and participated in the violence, but those in charge of the police, the government and its executive head, could avoid being held responsible. Such a judgement has wide-reaching implications, particularly when there are 'double engine' governments, a self-description by BJP leaders of the perfect scenario for them when their party runs both the central and state government. For example, what are the implications of this judgement on what is happening in Manipur? In Gujarat it was a week of violence. In Manipur, it raged for months. (The situation is not 'normal' as this book goes to press.) Is the state government and its executive head responsible for the situation or not?

Accountability as a principle of governance is also linked to justice. Victims of violence, particularly women, face numerous hurdles in the fight for justice in crimes committed against them. When the government is not held accountable it provides impunity to criminals who have often acted with the complicity and patronage, if not at the behest of parties running the government. This is true of Gujarat 2002. It is equally true of Manipur 2023.

2. Ethnic and Communal Majoritarianism in Manipur

I thought of Bilkis when I was in Manipur in August 2023. The Supreme Court was hearing her case the day I reached Manipur. I learnt that the court had asked pertinent questions about the basis of the earlier Supreme Court judgement which had opened the path for the subsequent remissions. How would this affect the women in Manipur, I wondered. I was in Manipur along with P.K. Srimati, the national president of AIDWA, and Mariam Dhawale, the national general secretary, on a mission of solidarity with the women of Manipur against the terrible violence which had started on May 3, 2023, and which had engulfed their beautiful state. We were there also to meet the victims of sexual assault and to extend to them our support and assistance.

More than three months later, the state was far from 'normal' and the fires of social and political division were raging in peoples' hearts. But there was also utter bewilderment, among scores of people we met, from both the Meitei and Kuki-Zomi communities, as to how such violence had occurred. They found it difficult to come to terms with the reality that people from the same village, including neighbours, who had lived together for years, could suddenly become foes. We also heard stories of how one community's members had saved the other. People, and especially women, of both communities were very seriously affected, thousands having had their homes burnt, living in appalling conditions in the relief camps. It is estimated that 69,000 people have been displaced due to the violence in which around 179 people have been killed, the majority of them from the Kuki-Zomi communities, the majority of whom are Christian.[12] Livelihoods are severely affected. Unorganized sector workers and, in particular, women in the handloom sector, were without any means of income. We were told by many women in Imphal that they were able to eat only once a day because the prices were extremely high with supplies being stopped due to blockades, and the utter failure of the government to intervene. We were told that families have had to take loans at usurious rates to survive, given the lack of work. It was bad enough in the Imphal valley, but when we went to the hill areas, the devastation and conditions of the people was much worse. There is little doubt that the tribals of Manipur—the Kuki-Zomi communities—bore the main brunt of the violence.

To understand the egregious, horrific violence against women that became known only weeks after it was committed, it is important to look at the larger context of politics and violence that enabled and covered it up. While admittedly, there are also historical factors behind the present situation in Manipur, we found from our discussions with hundreds of citizens of the state, from different communities, that they believed the blatant partisanship of the present BJP government, and in particular of its chief minister, to be the main cause behind the violence.

There has been a long-standing demand of the people of the valley, mainly comprising of the Meitei community, to access the land in the hills. A related demand has been to declare the Meitei community a Scheduled Tribe. The hill areas are presently protected by Article 371C of the Constitution which provides for the establishment of a Hill Council and protection of hill areas for the tribal population. Already, the Manipur government had started forcible evictions in thirty-eight villages in the hill areas claiming that these were occupied by 'illegal immigrants from Myanmar'. Despite several residents possessing proof of occupation for decades, the eviction commenced by conspicuously circumventing the due process. Under India's Constitution and legal framework, tribal communities and traditional forest dwellers have specific rights. All this was ignored. We were also told that the presence of mineral and oil deposits was another reason for the government's interest in greater control of hill areas. Several MOUs have been signed with corporates. Thus, corporate interest is also believed to be an important factor behind the official move to control the forest hill areas.

The trigger was a Manipur High Court direction to the government to expedite its recommendation regarding the demand to include the Meitei community in the ST list to the appropriate authorities. The Supreme Court later strongly criticized this direction as being entirely out of the jurisdiction of the High Court, but the damage had already been done. A big procession was held by tribal students' organizations against the High Court judgement. Clashes took place resulting in violence, loot, burning of houses, driving out of communities from each other's areas of dominance, killings, and also the most horrendous cases of sexual assault. Militant groups from both sides led the violence against each other. The difference between them being that in this round of violence, the state government led by Biren Singh not only defended but actually facilitated the looting of arms and ammunition, from the armouries of the Manipur police, by the armed militants whose members belonged to the Meitei community. Most members of this community have converted to Hinduism from their original Sanamahi beliefs. So, in both respects—ethnic as well as religious identity—the Meiteis are the majority community.

The chief minister led a campaign of calumny against the Kuki-Zomi communities. As stated at the outset, the majority of these communities are Christian. Somewhat similar to the language used against Muslim communities by top leaders of the BJP in mainland India, such as describing them as 'illegal immigrants' if they happen to be Bengali-speaking Muslims, or as 'termites' to be exterminated, in Manipur, the entire Kuki community was designated as illegal immigrants from Myanmar, as 'narco-terrorists' and 'criminals' that needed to be driven out of the state. A hate-based campaign by those in power against the minority Kuki Christian tribal communities marked the violence in Manipur. Threats were made to drive out all Kukis—a kind of ethnic cleansing.

In 2019, prior to the Lok Sabha elections, the BJP

had initiated talks with the militant Christian Kuki groups. According to an affidavit filed with the National Investigation Agency (NIA) in an ongoing case, Kuki leaders had described meetings they had held with Assam Chief Minister Himanta Biswa Sarma and RSS leader Ram Madhav, in which they were promised some concessions on their demands in lieu of Kuki votes for the BJP. In the assembly elections held in February–March 2022, the BJP won 37 of the 60 seats including seven of the ten seats in the Kuki-dominated hill areas. Following the violence, all ten Kuki MLAs have denounced the Biren Singh government and demanded a separate administration. The eight Naga MLAs, from a community which has remained 'neutral' during the ongoing violence, have opposed this demand and supported the Manipur government's stand of no separation of administration. With all these complexities and differing perceptions, what emerges from all the opinions expressed is the urgent requirement for a political solution, for a dialogue between communities, to which the present chief minister is seen as the biggest hurdle. Thus, demands for his resignation resonate across communities.

A crucial factor in all these developments has been the effort of the BJP and RSS to deploy a majoritarian framework in a sensitive state like Manipur, based on cultivating the Hindutva ideology among the Meitei community. Whether these efforts are successful or not, the attempt itself has very serious implications and repercussions. One can get an idea of the approach through RSS publications. A whole issue of its English-language publication, *Organiser*, dated May 21, 2023, repeats the slanderous charges against the

Kuki-Zomi tribal communities. An article states that 'more than 50,000 Chin Kukis from Myanmar have illegally sneaked in to Manipur... [T]hey are all fanatic Christians... burning Meitei Hindu villages and gunning [Meiteis] down... Meitei Hindus are patriotic people and resisting Christian conversion... Manipur for Christ is their target in line with Nagaland for Christ...'[13] These are the kind of lies and venom which have been directed at the Christian tribal communities by RSS shakhas functioning in Manipur, trying to consolidate their hold among the Meitei in the name of a Hindutva religious identity.

Against this background of hate-creation, rumours were deliberately floated that Meitei women had been raped in Churachandpur, a Kuki-Zomi area. We met Meitei women who genuinely believed these rumours and said that whatever had happened was a result of Meitei women being raped by Kuki men. The chief minister himself said that 'hundreds of such incidents had taken place'. The rumours were deliberate lies circulated to inflame passions. There were no cases of rape in Churachandpur, a fact confirmed also by the district commissioner to our delegation, but the chief minister has not retracted his statement. If indeed there were 'hundreds of such incidents' it is all the more reason for him to quit, having failed not only to prevent them but also to have done nothing for the hundreds of women so affected.

These responses were made after the horrific video surfaced of a young girl and an older woman, both belonging to the tribal communities, being stripped, molested and paraded by a cheering mob comprising men from the Meitei community. The younger woman was raped. While we were in Manipur, we learnt of the case of a Meitei woman who had filed an FIR stating that she had been sexually assaulted. We went to the police station to try and obtain details so that we could meet the victim. But we were denied access. Since then, there have been reports of a young Meitei girl student and her friend allegedly abducted by Kuki militants. Their brutalized bodies were found. It is reported that the girl was raped before being killed. That such a condemnable atrocity could occur months after the initial rounds of violence shows the utter failure of the central and state governments. The accused in this case, which led to outrage across the valley, were fortunately arrested quite swiftly. Yet the video evidence in the earlier cases of sexual assault of Kuki women has not been evidence enough to ensure the arrest of all those involved. Questions about double standards in ensuring justice are in order.

We met three of the victims of sexual assault and the parents of two girls who were believed to have been raped before being killed. We met some of them in Kangpokpi and others in Churachandpur, or Lamka, as the residents call it. The girls were being helped by Kuki and Zomi women's organizations that have provided counselling, shelter, support and solidarity to the victims, in the complete absence of government support. The girls are in deep trauma. Yet they reminded us to tell the world of what they had been through.

The young woman shown in the video was just twenty-one years old. The older woman was in her forties. On May 3, their village, B Phainom, was surrounded by a mob of Meitei men. They were among a group which fled the village. On the way they came across a group of policemen in a jeep and rushed to ask them for help. The driver told them they did not have the key to the jeep. They were literally handed over to the mob. This is what we learnt. The group got separated but the two women were taken together. They were forced to take off their clothes. The young brother of Y came rushing forward and clutched on to his sister, begging the crowd to let her go. The siblings hugged each other tight, weeping and pleading. He was literally torn away from her and killed before her eyes. Her father also tried to save his children and he too was killed. The two women were subjected to unspeakable sexual harassment. The younger woman was taken by a group of men and gang raped. Later, the army took them to a relief camp.

The camp was in an appalling condition, overcrowded and with no facilities. There was no privacy amidst hundreds of desperate families, all of whom had been forcibly displaced, many of their homes burnt. In these terrible conditions, the young woman, a victim of brutality, met her devastated and distraught mother in the camp. The mother had been away from the village and came to know about the killing of her son and husband later. She did not know what had happened to her daughter. For days the young woman could not share with her mother, or with anyone else, what she had gone through. She was overcome with the grief over the killing of her beloved younger brother and father, who she knew had been killed while trying to save her, but she did not want to burden her mother with her own trauma. And so, she kept silent. It was only days later that she spoke about the brutality she had experienced. The silence, the grief, the trauma took a heavy toll. She could not sleep or eat for weeks. She developed body tremors which affected her mobility.

An FIR was filed a fortnight later but the police and administration did not bother to contact her or the older woman. No action was taken on their complaints. In July, she learnt of the video which had gone viral, that the violence against her had been filmed and shared across the world. It was a grave setback to her recovery. The older woman said it was like being assaulted, humiliated all over again. The women say they know that most of the men who committed the crimes are free men, only a few have been arrested. The mother hoped to get the bodies of her son and husband back, which lay in a mortuary in Imphal and were therefore inaccessible. After several failed attempts, and finally through a court intervention, the bodies, along with those of others who belonged to tribal communities, were brought back to Churachandpur for the last rites and finally buried.

The third victim we met was a young tribal girl just fifteen years old. On May 15, she had gone to an ATM where she was abducted by a group of men in black uniforms, like those of the militant groups. They were all armed. They gang raped her and threw her down a hill. She survived and was taken to a military camp. When we met her, she could barely speak. Her family too despairs of getting justice. Other victims or their families whom we met had their own dreadful experiences to narrate. But each of them believed that the perpetrators would get away with their crimes because of political patronage and because they, the victims, were Christian and belonged to the Kuki-Zomi communities.

Some Questions that Arise

The Internal Logic of Majoritarianism

These women in Manipur were targeted because of their ethnic and religious identity, just as Bilkis was targeted because of her religious identity. The internal logic of a majoritarian framework of politics is such that what starts off as demonization of a particular community soon extends to other communities who do not fit into the majoritarian framework. Manipur teaches us that a communal majoritarian model being imposed by the BJP across the country has serious implications for women.

Dehumanizing Women

There is another striking lesson from Manipur, which is the dehumanizing impact such politics has on women. Manipur has been known for the strength of its women and the organizations run by Meitei women leaders and groups. For decades they have resisted state repression. In 2004, the image of twelve Manipuri women stripping in protest against the rape, torture and killing of a young woman shook the country.

Protests had been organized in many places and I too had organized and joined demonstrations against that horrible custodial atrocity. A write-up in *The Print* (July 22, 2021) recalls the incident: 'The women were protesting against the brutal killing of Manorama Thangjam, a 32-year-old woman who had been picked up by Assam Rifles personnel. Manorama's bullet-riddled body—with gunshot wounds to her private parts and thighs—was found near a paddy field hours after she was taken away from her home. Semen stains reportedly found on her clothes in a forensic exam suggested she had been raped. A judicial commission set up to look into the case painted a scathing account of torture that Manorama allegedly suffered in her final hours. The case proved a flashpoint in Manipur, where anger against the Armed Forces Special Powers Act (AFSPA 1958)—which allows use of force in certain situations in disturbed areas—was already pervasive. At the time, activist Irom Sharmila was already four years into a hunger strike against AFSPA that would last until 2016.'[14] The Imas (mothers) held up banners that said 'Indian Army Rape Us', and 'we are all Manorama'.

Particularly in a historical context of powerful resistance against the instrument of rape being used by the state to subdue dissident populations, it is especially disturbing to observe the lack of voices from women's groups in the valley protesting or condemning the sexual brutality against Kuki-Zomi women in the current conflict. It is true that the Meira Paibis, the powerful locality-based women's organizations in the Imphal valley, work independently of each other, though they have similar goals. During our trip to Manipur, we saw thousands of women patrolling their neighbourhoods in Imphal at night, holding their popular symbol of burning torches. Their slogans were against the

Assam Rifles, demanding that the force be withdrawn from Manipur on the ground that they were partial to the Kuki-Zomi communities. We were told that it was compulsory for each family to send a member to join the night watch. It was a display of strength and unity. But with all this strength, there was not a word or action against the sexual assault on tribal women. This is what communal and ethnic politics does to women too—it has a dehumanizing impact and develops a culture that justifies rape of the identified 'other'.

As mentioned earlier, there have been many incidents where neighbours and ordinary folk saved those caught in the crossfire. Sometimes in a single incident the victim experienced both things. This was experienced by two young nursing students who were trapped in their hostel. They were hidden for hours by their young Meitei colleagues. But when a mob of men entered the hostel, demanding all Kuki women come out, a group of Meitei women who were with the mob, started searching the rooms, found them and handed them over to the mob. Even then, the vice principal, a Meitei herself, did her utmost to save the girls, risking her own safety and positioning herself between the girls and the mob. She called the police. But the girls could not be protected. They were handed over to the mob, paraded, their hair pulled, beaten with sticks and rods—one of them suffered a serious head injury—abused in filthy sexist language and left for dead. One of the girls said that a group of women with the mob were shouting 'rape them, rape them, do what their men did to our women'. Later, they were found by the army and had to be admitted in the ICU of a government hospital.

One Point Agenda: Hindutva, Not Justice

In situations such as in Manipur, where sections of people indeed disapprove of the violence, the role of the government is critical. Do the actions and words of government leaders and the administration strengthen such disapproval and isolate the perpetrators of violence, thus helping to cut off support from the community? In the case of Manipur, the politics of those who govern is actually designed to create a majoritarian mindset to justify the violence against the communities targeted. The aim being consolidation of the Hindutva identity through the Meitei community, there was no move by the government to launch any initiative within the community to isolate the perpetrators of violence. The state government is not alone in its inaction. The deafening silence of the prime minister while Manipur burnt could be seen as a deliberate act, giving strength to the narrative of Hindutva—based on the ethnic and religious community identities in the state.

And when the PM did finally speak, one wished he hadn't. He trivialized the targeting of the Kuki-Zomi community, their horrors, by comparing what happened in Manipur to other incidents of violence in opposition-ruled states. Thus, it was not only the deliberate targeting of the Kuki-Zomi women and the nature of the crime against them that got short shrift from the prime minister. Victims of rape in the states named were demeaned by being turned into instruments for political point scoring.

Months later, the situation is still not normal. In the annual address delivered on the occasion of Dusschra in 2023, RSS chief Mohan Bhagwat gave a majoritarian-nationalist spin to the issue to conceal the utter failure of the Biren Singh government. In his speech, Bhagwat stated, 'Manipur is the work of outside forces who want to create divisions in India.' The prime minister boasts that it is his government alone which has protected India against 'outside forces'—one side of its fake nationalism. The other side of its fake nationalism is the accusation that 'it is outside forces [that are] responsible' every time his own government fails. A case of heads I win, tails you lose! But for the women of Manipur awaiting justice, a legitimate question would be: Is it outside forces who raped them? Is it outside forces that are protecting the criminals? Is it outside forces that are responsible for conducting an inquiry which is going nowhere? The wages of communal and ethnic majoritarianism are extracting a heavy price from the women of Manipur.

3. Communal Majoritarianism in 'Normal Times'

It is not just the targeting of Muslim or Christian women during communal strife that marks the drive towards a majoritarian India. It is equally the targeting of minority women during 'normal' times. What happened in January 2018 in Kathua, a village in Jammu, the victim an eight-year-old child, Asifa Bano? The chargesheet filed in that case was made public. Can any human being remain unmoved by the horrors that the child experienced, depicted so graphically in the chargesheet? Is there anyone who would not be filled with rage and abhorrence against the extreme brutalities committed by the accused? They were accused of abducting her, sedating her, raping her in turn, inviting an associate from Meerut to 'satisfy his lust', postponing the moment of her death because one of them 'wanted to rape her again'. But there were such people who were not only unmoved, but who strained every nerve, and it would seem every muscle, to subvert the processes of justice. These were not ordinary men. They are men who were ministers in the state government, men who lead organizations, men who wear the black robes of lawyers, those who are supposed to serve the ends of justice.

For two months following the arrests of six men including a temple priest, the area was witness to mobilizations and agitations organized by the Hindu Ekta Manch, a platform set up by affiliates of the Sangh Parivar, backed by the RSS. What was their agitation about? One may have thought they were agitated because the horrific crime took place in the prayer room of the local temple. Were these men on the streets because they wanted more stringent punishment against those who defiled a temple prayer room with their dastardly acts? Far from it. The Hindu Ekta Manch pursued just one aim—to prove that the investigation was wrong, the arrests were wrong because all those arrested happen to be Hindus whereas the child victim belonged to a Muslim family.

In Kathua, it isn't merely the case that the processes of justice post the rape and murder which were communalized and sought to be subverted. Shamefully, as the chargesheet shows, it was communal consideration that determined the selection of the victim as well. The rape was a deliberate plan to terrorize the Bakherwal community into leaving the area. The Bakherwals and the Gujjars, recognized as Scheduled Tribes, are Muslim by belief. The child was raped, according to the chargesheet, because she was a Muslim.

It was the most shameful display of communalization of crime, one, moreover, that involved a child victim. The criminals were convicted and given life sentences. Even in this case, while the horrendous crime and the shameful activities of the Hindutva eco-system led to nationwide protests by women's organizations and others, and even when the international press took note of it, the prime minister did not utter a word till three months later, in April. This attitude contradicts the claims made by the Modi government about its concern for children, which it sought to demonstrate by bringing an amendment to the IPC including the death sentence for the rape of children. I have already explained my opposition to the death sentence in principle, but here is a government amending the relevant law, the Protection of Children Against Sexual Offences (POCSO) Act (2012) to include the death penalty,[15] while in cases like Kathua, not only is the death penalty not invoked, every effort is made by the communal majoritarian eco-system to prove that such a crime was never even committed.

In 'normal' times, hate speech with demeaning references to Muslim women is common. Speeches by Sangh Parivar leaders, including those at so-called Dharma Sansads, or 'religious parliaments', amplify Savarkar's violent fantasies of wreaking revenge on Muslim women. After strong protests against a speech made in April 2022 at one such gathering, the offender, Bajrang Muni Das, the head of a temple in Sitapur, Uttar Pradesh, was arrested. While the arrest came two weeks after his call to rape Muslim women, Das was released on bail just a week later.

Open-source apps like 'Sulli Deals' and 'Bulli Bai' divulged personal details of prominent Muslim women in an 'online auction'. One of the targets, Hana Mohsin Khan, a pilot, told a reporter from *The Quint*, after a month of inaction from the government: 'No one is taking it seriously. The cops are letting it pass because the tag of Muslim women is attached. When a small account talks about any politician in a derogatory way, they are immediately arrested or taken to task. But men who take photos of women and are posting them online, they don't have resources to catch them? It is unbelievable. It is deliberate and they simply do not want to do it.' After Sulli Deals was taken down, a similar website, Bulli Bai was launched. For a year there were no arrests. This prompted the United Nations Special Rapporteur on Minority Issues, Fernand de Varennes, to state in January 2022, 'Minority Muslim women in India are harassed and "sold" in social media apps, #SulliDeals, a form of hate speech, must be condemned and prosecuted as soon as they occur. All Human rights of minorities need to be fully and equally protected.'[16] But there was no response, not a word from any government or BJP leader. The sites were traced to young male students, showing how the sexual targeting of Muslim women by the eco-system influences younger generations.

Demonization of Muslim Men

If Muslim women are to be the targets of revenge, and their bodies the site to avenge historical wrongs, real or imagined, the demonization of Muslim men is an equally if not more important aspect of the Hindutva project. Revenge can become a tool for mass mobilization if it can be shown that Hindu women are being sexually targeted by Muslim men today, that Muslim men are rapists and sexual harassers, by nature. The theory of 'love jihad' is an essential tool in this endeavour, which I describe later in this essay.

In 2018, a propagandist of the Hindutva eco-system, a

man called Mahesh Vikram Hegde, made the outrageous claim that Muslims accounted for 96 per cent of the rapes committed in the 2016–18 period. According to his self-declared profile, Hegde runs a foundation called Vikrama Foundation, news portals and channels. On July 23, 2018, he tweeted, '...from 2016-2018 a total of 84,374 rapes took place of which 81,000 rapists were Muslims, 96 percent of the women and children targeted by the rapists were Hindus. In [our] nation it is not Muslims in danger but Hindus'. The eco-system multiplied this toxic message through more than 1,200 swift retweets, and presumably, countless WhatsApp forwards. The information turned out to be totally doctored as several fact-checking websites proved. The figures did not match the number of registered rapes during those years as recorded by the National Crime Records Bureau. Nor is there any community-wise breakdown of rapists or their victims in any government database except for crimes against the Scheduled Castes and Scheduled Tribes. But the outrageous message multiplied by the eco-system had done the damage it sought to do, namely that rapes in India are because of Muslims. This is a man who declares on his Twitter account: 'Blessed to be followed by Narendra Modi.'

Violence Through Speech and Threats

In the protests against the Citizenship Amendment Act (CAA) which swept India in 2019, the Hindutva eco-system used the most abusive language against Muslim women participating in the protests. Shaheen Bagh, the protest site in north-east Delhi where there was an indefinite sit-in led by women, became the heroic epicentre of the protest. In the context of the Hindutva eco-system, Shaheen Bagh became a metaphor for toxic anti-minority hate speech.

In the run-up to the Delhi assembly elections, members of parliament Parvesh Verma and Anurag Thakur (then also Minister of State for Finance and Corporate Affairs) made vitriolic speeches. A recurrent theme reflected the cynical use of women's bodies for electoral purposes, namely, the threat of rape by Muslims. Verma said: 'Lakhs of people gather there [Shaheen Bagh]. People of Delhi will have to think and take a decision. They'll enter your houses, rape your sisters and daughters, and kill them. There's time today, Modiji and Amit Shah won't come to save you tomorrow... The people know that a fire engulfed Kashmir in which their mothers and sisters were raped. This happened in Kerala, Uttar Pradesh, Hyderabad.'[17] Such mistruths were spread with ease. They had the support of the top leadership of the party. In a letter to the prime minister, signed by 170 activists, women's organizations and groups asked him: 'What is this kind of communal hate and fear-mongering that you, as a head of government, are encouraging, that seeks to make women of all communities feel more insecure and threatened? Vote for BJP or you will get raped! Is this your election message to Delhi's women? Is this how low your party has sunk?' The prime minister and home minister had themselves targeted Shaheen Bagh.

The Election Commission, in a mild reprimand, banned Verma and Thakur from campaigning for a few days. But the Delhi police refused to take cognisance of the crime. Since

January 2020, when I had filed a case against Verma and Thakur with the police, not even an FIR has been registered. The complaint has moved from court to court but no action has been taken yet. Such impunity has encouraged and emboldened other BJP leaders to run election campaigns on similar lines.

Before the Gujarat state assembly elections in 2023, the horrific murder case of a young woman, Shraddha Walkar, by her live-in partner Aftab Poonawala was widely reported. This criminal had murdered Shraddha and then cut up her body into pieces, and even before he had disposed of her mutilated body parts stored in the refrigerator, he had invited another girl to his apartment. It was a horrendous crime. But resorting to the same language as Parvesh Verma who had escaped any punishment, the Assam chief minister, Himanta Biswa Sarma, while campaigning for the Gujarat elections in December 2022, stated: 'Vote for Modi—without a strong leader in the country, murderers like Aftab will emerge in every city and we will not be able to save our society.'[18] Sarma forgot that the horrendous murder took place in the capital of India, a city where the police is directly under the Modi government. What he said was no different from what Vikram Hegde had said, equating Muslims with rapists. For the Assam chief minister, Aftabs—Muslims—are murderers of women who only Modi can stop.

In fact, the Shraddha Walkar case is not just about the character of her murderer. The brutality and inhumanity involved in her murder and the dismemberment of her body point also to the utter vulnerability of a young woman trapped in a relationship with a serial abuser. The testimonies of her well-wishers and colleagues revealed that Shraddha had spoken of repeated subjection to violence at the hands of Poonawala. Yet their attempts to extract her out of that toxic relationship did not succeed. The evidence of violence against her was never shared with the police. These are the issues which must concern society—what, for example, are the cultures which enable men's violence in relationships and disable women's responses? But in communalizing the identity of the killer, basic issues are obscured. This too is part of the eco-system of the Hindutva votaries.

This demonization is presented in the eco-system as a nationalist cause. When Muslims are depicted as criminals—rapists—it is a step away from proclaiming it a nationalist cause to fight Muslims, the fundamental RSS approach which links nationalism to religious identity. It was Savarkar, in his essay 'Essentials of Hindutva', who floated the theory that only those for whom the 'pitrabhum and punyabhum' (fatherland and holy land) were the same could be considered Bharatiyas.[19] This theory forever excludes Muslims as equal citizens because their centre of worship is Mecca, and Catholics, because the centre of worship is the Vatican. Hedgewar and Golwalkar, his successors in advancing the Hindutva ideology, stated that 'Muslims can live in India wholly subordinated to the Hindu nation'. They had identified the internal enemy as not only Muslims, but Christians and communists. This formed the basis for the subsequent assertions, common today, that only Hindus could be nationalists—Hindu nationalists as opposed to Indian nationalists, reflected in the slogan of 'cultural nationalism'. Under the present regime, this is extended to linking Muslims with every heinous crime, particularly concentrating on sexual crimes, and rousing fears that Muslims are a threat to the safety and security of Hindu women.

Most nationalisms use the woman as the symbol of a nation. The woman is always in need of protection and defence, just as the nation is. Here in India, a common reference is to the nation as Bharat Mata—Mother India. In the symbols of the Hindutva eco-system, Mother India is very prominently Hindu, resembling the image of a popular goddess. Hindu equals nation, Nation equals woman—thus Nation equals Hindu woman. It is the nation, the Hindu woman, who is threatened by Muslim men.

Hindutva Women

Savarkar's slogan of the 'militarization' of the 'Hindu race' is reflected in the promotion of masculinity as a core feature of Hindutva, the creation of the macho man, the eternal warrior, whose very existence is dependent on aggression against the identified foe; whose every action must be imbued with the spirit of avenging 'historical wrongs'; for whom every non-Hindu must be viewed as a potential enemy of the nation until the non-Hindu redeems himself by accepting the crimes of his forefathers and atones for them by subordinating himself to whatever punishment is meted out to him. Conversely, the belief is fostered that no Hindu can ever be a 'terrorist' but must always be thought of as a man with the highest of virtues, especially if he is a Brahmin. Savarkar, in the essay quoted above (*Six Glorious Epochs of*

Indian History),[20] makes a scathing critique of Buddhism because it preached ahimsa and universal brotherhood. He wrote of 'the necessity of creating a bitter sense of wrong, invoking a power of undying resistance especially in India that had under the opiates of Universalism and non-violence lost the faculty even of resisting sin and crime and aggression'. He spoke of the need of 'political and masculine virility'. Decades later, this 'necessity of creating a bitter sense of wrong' can be observed in the current attempts to rewrite India's history as an endless war between Hindus and Muslims. RSS chief Mohan Bhagwat in an interview to the *Organiser* said: 'Hindu society has been at war for over 1,000 years... [I]t is but natural for those at war to be aggressive... [T]his war is not against an outside enemy, but against an enemy within. So there is a war to defend Hindu society, Hindu Dharma and Hindu culture...'[21] One may add—going by current practice—that in this war, women of the identified 'other' are easy, soft targets to demonstrate 'masculine virility'. There is another aspect to this. The masculinization of Hindutva, which is an essential part of this project based as it is on violence, has a direct impact on the movement's mobilization of women.

In the drive towards a majoritarian India, there are two objectives of this women's mobilization. The first is the direct participation of women in aggressive Hindutva drills. The second is reiterating the central role of the 'family' and the designated position of the ideal wife and mother in Hindutva's cultural-nationalist narrative. The Rashtra Sevika Samiti was formed in 1936 to fulfil both these roles.

One may note how, across the world, often associated

with right-wing politics is the stereotypical image of a passive woman. Ironically, the avenues opened up for all women by women's movements for radical social change have influenced right-wing organizational structures leading to the promotion of women. Thus, we see women emerge as leaders of right-wing parties, spewing hate, as in the white supremacist politics in the United States or the anti-immigrant mobilizations in Europe. In Islamist societies, we see women leaders committed to fundamentalist ideologies, defending the subordinate role of women in patriarchal interpretations of religious scriptures. Here in India, the anti-minority hate speeches backed by mobilizations of the lynching mobs, are often led and provoked by right-wing women leaders, patronized by those in power.

During the nineties, pre and post the Babri Masjid demolition, women such as Sadhvi Rithambara and Uma Bharti led the deeply anti-Muslim campaign with the filthiest of abuse. Since then, many other such women leaders have emerged. Their interventions are based in equal part on hate against the identified target, vocal reverence for a sectarian view of nationalism defined by religion and custom, and the glorification of the traditional roles of women expressed in their participation in and propagation of rituals, many of which are deeply male-centric. More recently, young women are being organized and trained in the use of batons and even swords, demonstrated in women's marches during religious festivals, accompanied by provocative sloganeering against minorities. For example, the Ram Navami processions in Bengal saw unprecedented scenes of young girls wielding swords and aggressively shouting provocative slogans. In the

Dharma Sansads, women speakers deliver the most hate-filled provocative speeches. Pragya Thakur, an accused in the 2008 bomb blast that killed at least six people in Malegaon, who praised Gandhi's murderer Godse, is an example of such a woman. A serial offender who asks 'Hindus' to keep weapons in their homes, and 'at least keep the knives used to cut vegetables sharp'[22] to defend themselves, was not just elected on a BJP ticket, but has the patronage of top leaders of the party. This is a direct encouragement to other women in the Parivar who believe they can gain prominence, like Pragya Thakur, through hate crimes and speeches. A BJP Mahila Morcha office bearer in Uttar Pradesh, Sunita Singh Gaur, posted on Facebook in June 2019: 'There is only one solution for them [Muslims]. Hindu brothers should make a group of ten and gangrape their [Muslims'] mothers and sisters openly on the streets...and then hang her in the middle of the bazaar for others to see'. The lady in question was subsequently removed from her post by her party after strong protests, but she was protected from prosecution for hate speech by the UP government.[23]

In a Dharma Sansad held in Raipur in December 2021, another so-called sadhvi—a female renunciate—Vibhanand Giri urged the men present to 'rape and impregnate Muslim women if Muslim men cast even a glance at Hindu girls' and that if Muslim men even look at Hindu girls, it would lead to 'their' women 'producing babies from Hindus without marriage'.[24] Nupur Sharma whose vulgar comments against Prophet Mohammed made international news, which forced the BJP to sack her, was strongly supported by the Hindutva eco-system and protected from criminal action.

Dedicated to the one-point agenda of militant Hindutva, women spewing hate, asking their men to rape Muslim women, are the opposite of empowered women—they do as they are told in the Hindutva family. This is as true of top BJP women leaders who, as ministers in the Modi government, have never criticized such statements—never, not even once.

It is in this context of the creation of an aggressive Hindutva women's contingent that the RSS, according to its chief Mohan Bhagwat, in its centenary year, is actively considering direct membership to women in the RSS. In his interview, Bhagwat mentioned that while there is a Rashtra Sevika Samiti, women are more inspired by the RSS and want direct membership of the organization. This would not mean the breaking of a male bastion—far from it. It is not to fight patriarchy, dowry deaths, increasing sexual assault on women and children or against brutal acts of domestic violence that women are being inducted. The shakha will act as the womb to produce more hate-spewing women.

Manuvadi Majoritarianism

Manuvadi majoritarianism differentiates between a woman raped by a Muslim and one by a Hindu. In the former case, as we have seen, it is the religious identity of the criminal which is highlighted, and the eco-system goes into action. But in the latter case, it is the woman herself who is to be blamed. Only bad women get raped. Only women who wear revealing clothes get raped. Only women who are out late at night get raped. Only women who are out with male friends get raped. Good women who obey rules don't get raped. Be a good woman and escape rape!

It is not just the RSS-BJP which deploys such language. Misogynist leaders across the political spectrum have made objectionable statements. But certainly, it can be said that the strongest upholders of such misogyny in the most sustained way have been, and are, the modern Manuvadis of the Sangh Parivar. Control over a woman's sexuality as ordained by the *Manusmriti* is the basic DNA of the eco-system, because women are by nature corrupt. The *Manusmriti* says: 'It is the very nature of women to corrupt men here on earth; for that reason, circumspect men do not get careless and wanton among wanton women' (Chapter 2, Verse 213).

Mohan Bhagwat's infamous statement in January 2013, that 'rapes happen only in India and not Bharat',[25] came soon after the horrific Nirbhaya rape. He said: 'You go to villages and forests of the country and there will be no such incidents of gang-rape or sex crimes. They are prevalent in some urban belts. Besides new legislations, Indian ethos and attitude towards women should be revisited in the context of ancient Indian values.' The 'ancient Indian values' were described by his colleague, a prominent Hindutva votary, Kailash Vijayvargiya, then Minister for Industries in the BJP government in Madhya Pradesh, a few days later: 'One has to abide by certain moral limits. If you cross this limit, you will be punished, just like Sita was abducted by Ravana.'[26] In this statement by a man who was then minister, Sita was a woman who had 'crossed moral limits'—a bad woman—and so, was punished. Following protests, the BJP national leadership distanced itself from this statement—not from the man who made it, who was once again made a minister in the Madhya Pradesh government in 2023—but it does show the mentality of the Hindutva leaders.

The communalization of sexual violence serves yet another purpose. It deflects attention from this aspect of Hindutva—its patriarchal, Manuvadi framework. In fact, crimes against women have seen a consistent rise in the years of BJP rule.

Increase in Crimes Against Women

The BJP's election manifesto in 2014 stated that under the previous Congress-led United Progressive Alliance government 'crimes against women have reached unacceptable levels'. It mentioned the 'gross misuse and total denigration of government and institutions'. The Nirbhaya case was critical in their narrative. It pledged to reverse this record. How far has the BJP government, under the leadership of Narendra Modi, lived up to its pledge?

Registered cases of violence against women in India are officially collated by the nodal agency functioning under the central government—the National Crime Records Bureau (NCRB). The range of crimes is registered under around thirty different 'heads' reflecting the legal framework of the Indian Penal Code (IPC) and Special Local laws (SLL) and ranges from sexual harassment, rape, gang rape, domestic violence, dowry deaths, abduction, acid attacks, trafficking.

In 2018, a survey conducted by the Thomas Reuters Foundation found India to be the 'most unsafe place for women'. The Modi government rejected the methodology as unscientific, calling it an effort to 'malign the nation'. In 2013, when India was ranked fourth in the TRF survey, leaders of the BJP used the report to slam the then UPA government. A methodology which was fine to quote in 2013, becomes a slur on India five years later. Be that as it may, the data put out by the NCRB shows a most alarming picture of the increase in violence in over nine years of BJP rule. In 2014, when the BJP took over the reins of government, crimes against women rose by 9.2 per cent compared to 2013. A total of 3,37,922 cases of crime against women were reported in the country during that year as compared to 3,09,546 in the previous year, 2013. Between 2014 and 2023, the number of crimes against women rose to 4.45 lakh registered crimes, an increase of over 28 per cent. More than fifty cases of crime against women were lodged on an average every single hour. The rate of crime, committed against women per lakh population, increased from 56.3 per cent to 64.5 per cent in 2021 and further to 66.4 per cent in 2022. The NCRB reports a further increase in crimes against women by 4 per cent in its report of December 2023. It further flags a concern that while the general crime rate in India has declined, the rate in crimes against women has increased.

The largest number of these registered cases, almost 32 per cent, relate to domestic violence and abuse. Over 18 per cent of the cases are of sexual harassment, euphemistically and wrongly described in the law as well as in official documentation as cases of 'outraging the modesty of women'. It is not 'outraging modesty', it is a criminal assault on the bodily integrity of a woman—sexual harassment—

but governments prefer to obfuscate the reality of the crime by the use of words like 'modesty'. It is not just a question of semantics. It is this mindset which gets reflected in blaming the woman victim of sexual harassment for what she experiences because of her 'lack of modesty'. Crimes of sexual assault also show an increasing trend. In 2022, India registered 31,982 cases of rape—which means that on an average, every day nearly eighty-eight women were victims of rape who registered a case. Of these victims of rape, on an average four were Adivasi and eleven were Dalit. Almost ten per cent of rape victims were minors. The Family Health Survey which, on the basis of a questionnaire, conducts a house-to-house survey, shows that a large number of women victims of sexual violence do not register cases for various reasons. So, these figures, which are bad enough, still do not depict the full picture.

Low Conviction Rates

An important question is whether the police and judicial systems can ensure the certainty of punishment. This is an issue that women's organizations and movements have been most concerned about. In India, a variety of factors including class, caste and community are involved in the denial of justice to victims of rape. Typically, the conviction rate in cases where the victim is a poor woman and one belonging to an oppressed caste is low; such victims find it much more difficult to access justice. Conviction rates in cases of sexual assault are dismal to begin with. Not only are there very high rates of pendency before various levels of the judicial system, but the conviction rate itself is between 20 and 25 per cent only—which means that of every hundred men accused of rape, seventy-five walk free. Information furnished in the Lok Sabha in March 2020 disclosed that as of December 2019, there were 2.44 lakh cases related to rape and the POCSO Act pending in courts. Promises for fast-track courts have not helped in most cases. While the government had proposed to set up a total of 1,023 such courts, only around 40 per cent have been set up and are functioning. If justice delayed is justice denied then India's women victims of sexual assault and domestic violence are on a long and hard road.

These facts show that there has been government failure at both levels—that of prevention of crime as well as punishment for the crime. While other governments in the past, too, have had poor records in stemming the tide of violence and abuse of women, under the RSS-led BJP rule, there is a qualitative difference. This lies in the conservative and orthodox cultural framework of the Sangh Parivar based on the *Manusmriti*, which comes into direct conflict with the constitutional recognition of a woman as an independent citizen with equal rights.

Autonomy vs Patriarchal Control

An instance of this cultural framework is that women who are in consensual relations, or display behaviour that is considered 'immoral', are considered legitimate targets to be taught a lesson by the Manuvadi eco-system. They fit into the category of women to be punished. It often becomes a case of women's autonomy versus control over her sexuality.

In November 2023, a young woman student walking in the Benares Hindu University (BHU) campus with a male friend at night was surrounded by a gang of men, who beat up the man, abused the woman of being a 'loose' woman and told her she had to be taught a lesson. She was stripped, videoed, raped. This is the world of vigilantism promoted by Hindutva cultures.

There are different types of vigilantism, one of them being against 'wayward' women.

Arbitrary vigilantism—the 2009 Sri Ram Sena attack on pub-goers in Bangalore, or lathi-wielding men pouncing on young couples celebrating Valentine's Day in UP—perceived as 'fringe action' before BJP's ascendancy, has now become mainstream.

In UP, 'anti-Romeo' squads—police detachments raised to curb instances of sexual harassment—often assisted by accompanying gangs of men owing allegiance to the Sangh Parivar, routinely apprehended young romancing couples. According to a response to a Right to Information (RTI) application filed by *India Today*,[27] between November 2020 and March 2021, as many as 14,454 arrests were made, an average of eleven arrests a day, an alarmingly high number. Yet UP is a state with high crime rates against women. While actions against sexual harassment are welcome, it is reported that in many cases it was vigilante groups, which have appointed themselves for the purpose of moral policing, who guided the police squads. Hundreds of cases were reported where, in the name of curbing sexual harassment, young couples were caught and humiliated, young women threatened that their parents would be informed. Indeed, the dark side of the moral policing is the sexual violence against a young woman as punishment for being in a consensual relationship, more so if it is expressed in the public domain. Conservative opinions about autonomy of young adults to make their own choices gets translated into government policy, unleashing social forces that consider such women as 'bad' and in need of punishment.

When such patriarchal and misogynist thinking and practice is combined with casteist supremacy it constitutes one of the worst forms of backlash against Indian women who have fought for and won many rights.

Some cases emerge as the symbols of Manuvadi majoritarianism, but as well of the resistance against it. The Hathras case of 2020 is one such, as is the case of the female wrestlers in 2023.

Hathras: Metaphor for Manuvadi Injustice

Hathras is etched in indelible letters at the juncture of caste, class and gender in the framework of Manuvadi majoritarianism. On September 14, 2020, a nineteen-year-old Dalit girl in the Boolgarhi village of Hathras district of UP was found unconscious in a neighbouring field by her mother, her clothes in disarray, bleeding from the mouth. She fought for her life for fifteen days. Before succumbing to her injuries in a hospital on September 29, she made a statement, legally accepted as her dying declaration, in which she named four men who she said had gang raped and then beat her and left her for dead. After her death, the district magistrate and the police forcibly took away her body from her family and cremated her in the dead of night. The girl belonged to a family of poor agricultural workers in a village dominated by landowning classes. By community, the majority are Thakur, the same caste as the chief minister of the state. The four men, Sandeep, Ramu, Luv Kush and Ravi, named by her all belonged to Thakur families.

From the day this caste-based atrocity occurred, the BJP-RSS eco-system went into overdrive to subvert the processes of justice to deny the young woman a chance to survive or even to die with dignity. I visited her family on October 5, as part of a delegation of Left parties to offer solidarity and support. In that small dark room, a few women were huddled together, cradling her mother, Rama Devi. Her two sisters and her brothers sat weeping in the corner, repeating the horror of the atrocity. What I sensed in the palpable grief and sadness in that small space was a rage against injustice but it was a rage that was suppressed by the structure of caste-produced helplessness. Members of the family were virtually under house arrest. No one was allowed to meet them without the permission of the authorities. In our cultures, death brings with it mourners, crowds of people who throng the house of the deceased to express their sorrow and solidarity. Not so in Hathras. Sympathy for the Dalit family was seen as a political challenge to the dominant caste; even collective mourning was seen as a protest. They had no right to accuse Thakur boys of rape. If indeed there was sexual intercourse, it must have been consensual!

Ranjeet Bahadur Srivastava, a BJP leader from Uttar Pradesh's Barabanki, claimed that the nineteen-year-old woman was having an affair with the accused and called him to the millet field where she was found on September 14, and was then killed by her family. 'Such girls are found dead in only some places. They will be found dead in sugarcane, corn and millet fields or in bushes, gutters or forests...she was caught.'[28] The BJP MLA from Ballia constituency, Surendra Singh, said in a statement that rapes can only be stopped if parents teach daughters to behave decently.[29] The language—'such girls' or 'teach [them] to behave decently', implying the girl had behaved 'indecently'—is the kind you can find in verses of the *Manusmriti.*

This demeaning of a young Dalit woman and the public contempt displayed by top leaders of the BJP was not an example of male crassness but one of upper-caste assertion and entitlement. It was backed by casteist mobilizations by so-called upper-caste organizations like the notorious Karni Sena, claiming to represent 'Rajput pride', the Kshatriya Mahasabha, and the Rashtriya Savarna Sangathan. These mobilizations were permitted by the administration in support of the criminals. On reaching Hathras, we ourselves witnessed groups of young men with lathis, positioned at the entrance of the village and at almost every corner of it. When we asked officials how this was being allowed, they answered that it was an emotional response of the village against 'outsiders' disturbing the peace. In fact, it was to isolate, intimidate and threaten Dalits who may have wanted to mourn with the family. The family was effectively isolated. The organizers had the audacity to support criminals in the wake of such a horrendous atrocity because they knew that the UP government was fully backing them. Within a day of the atrocity being reported on social media, the authorities sprang into action to deny the crime had even taken place, with the district magistrate and UP government calling the report 'fake news'. The girl's forensic report was not prepared till ten days after she was sexually brutalized. After all the evidence was lost, a senior police officer used this as a pretext to declare to the press that there was no evidence of rape.

When outrage at the atrocity did not abate, the ecosystem led by the UP chief minister said it was 'a conspiracy against the state'. He further gave a call to party workers to protest. His government went further to file nineteen FIRs targeting those who had exposed its role in the matter, including a journalist from Kerala, Siddique Kappan, on charges like sedition, conspiracy to organize caste violence and so on. Kappan was on his way to Hathras coincidentally on the same day as our delegation. He was stopped on the way and charged under the Unlawful Activities (Prevention) Act (UAPA), before he had written a single line. But as noted by the Supreme Court, which granted him bail in 2022, even after two years, no formal charges were filed. He was also charged with unrelated crimes which again kept him in jail. He was finally granted bail in all cases only after spending twenty-eight months in jail. The chilling message from the UP government was: do as we say or face imprisonment.

The Hathras case was handed over to the CBI which charged the criminals with rape and murder. However, the Special Court hearing the case, disregarding the dying declaration of the victim, exonerated three of the accused, struck down charges of rape and sentenced only one of them, Sandeep, to life imprisonment. I was told recently by the brother of the victim that the UP government had refused to file an appeal in the case. The family themselves have had to go in appeal. The UP government, however, has gone in appeal against another judgement related to the case. The Allahabad High Court, taking suo motu cognisance of the atrocity, had issued orders in July 2022 to the government to provide compensation, a government job to a family member, and to provide a house to the family outside Hathras since they were extremely insecure. While 25 lakh rupees have been given to the family, the government's written assurance to provide a house and job has remained unfulfilled. The family filed four affidavits in the court to demand the UP government fulfil its promise.

Earlier governments, even if they sided with the elite, would use subterfuge to do it. Now even such pretence is dispensed with. The government wears its upper-caste bias on its sleeve. The victim's brother tells me that after the release of three of the accused, the pressure and threats against them have intensified. They cannot move out of their home. Hardly anyone visits them. Both brothers have been forced to give up their jobs because of death threats. They are under protection of armed police and cannot move out without them. Thus, it is not just that they lost their beloved sister, but they are being punished for daring to fight, for refusing to compromise and they suffer the consequences every minute, every day. This is the face of Manuvad.

Dalit women in India have a history of resistance and struggle. They are the untouchables who Manu's laws consider so low by birth that they are outside the caste system, with no voice, no rights, forever slaves, born to serve the upper castes. The sexual violence visited on Dalit women through the course of history is perhaps the most invisibilized endemic, structural sexual violence any community the world over has faced. Manu's laws, applied to Dalit women, sanctioned every act as 'service' to the upper caste in the varnashrama dharma. Adivasi women too have been historically appropriated within this category of untouchables by the caste hierarchy.

I recall listening to Godavari Parulekar, legendary leader and organizer of the Warli Adivasis in Thane district of Maharashtra, speak about the endemic nature of sexual violence Adivasi women had to face from the landlords and moneylenders of the area. In her book *Adivasis Revolt*[30] she writes, 'Landlords considered their tenants wives and the wives of their debt slaves to be their personal property. They firmly believed that they had the hereditary right to enjoy these women whenever it pleased them to do so. It was a common thing for them to make obscene remarks to the women who worked for them, to touch them, to pinch them, push them alone into a corner and molest them...' Writing on the Telangana armed struggle against the trinity of the Nizam of Hyderabad, the Razakars and the landlords, foremost communist leader of the struggle, P. Sundarayya, in a chapter in his book on the role of women, recounts, 'the women [Dalit and Adivasi labourers and poor peasants] were the worst victims of the torture and atrocities committed...

[T]hey had to face molestation and rape apart from beatings on a large scale... [T]he story of their resistance in defence of their personal dignity, against molestation, rape and torture is an inspiring one'.

These were experiences of Dalit and Adivasi women in the early and mid-twentieth century, where a hereditary right to sexually assault Dalit and ati-shudra women, as their own property, has been recorded, as has the resistance of those women. Their caste, their being part of an exploited class, and their being women united to turn Dalit women into upper-caste male property—for centuries of India's history. And all this had the sanction of Manu's laws.

When present-day rulers refer to India as the 'mother of democracy', they paper over the reality of the caste system, insult the lived experience for centuries of shudra and untouchable women in this our ancient land, violently coerced, from birth, into a system where their own bodies were not their own but the property of those higher up in the social ladder to use and discard at their will, never allowed to enjoy concepts like security, safety, choice.

We need to remember that history today, to prevent the deletion in our collective memory of the huge toll taken of human dignity and the dignity of women of the lower castes and classes by the monarchical feudal, casteist social structures which ruled India, for centuries before and during the Mughal regime and the British colonial regime. With the invisibilization of the increased power of casteist forces and structures under the rule of the modern Manuvadis, it is imperative today to remember, because eliminating that history is to repeat it. Hathras is not an isolated example—it is the brutal and bloody symbol of caste power protected by governments and the state. It is a shame and an indication of the power of Manuvadi cultures that the UP government has not been called out for exerting such bias. Neither has it been questioned on its utterly unjust and casteist refusal to appeal against the court judgement.

The Women Wrestlers

The most decorated women wrestlers of India still await justice. In January 2023, India was surprised when three medal-winning, well-known female wrestlers, Vinesh Phogat, Sakshi Malik and Anshu Malik, supported by decorated male wrestler, Bajrang Punia, led a group of young wrestlers in an indefinite sit-in at the capital's traditional protest site, Jantar Mantar. They were demanding action against the head of the Wrestling Federation of India, a powerful MP of the BJP, Brij Bhushan Sharan Singh. They accused him of serial sexual harassment, and asserted that despite their complaints to the authorities, no action had been taken against him, which was why they were forced to publicly protest.

On the third day of the dharna, I visited the site along with AIDWA activists in solidarity. While I was trying to navigate my way through the crowd towards where the women wrestlers were sitting, Bajrang Punia was incorrectly informed that I had come to address the gathering. He said something which was inaudible to me at the time, but this was captured by the scores of cameras at the site, and a story was put out that CPI(M) leader Brinda Karat was asked to leave the site. Punia had asked me to 'sit in front' as no political leaders were being asked to speak. Meanwhile, Sakshi Malik and other young women came forward to meet me and explained the reasons for their dharna. I stayed at the site for quite some time but the video and report went viral and pro-BJP trolls had a field day talking about how I had been 'snubbed'. I mention this minor matter only to illustrate that the ruling party was only concerned that the wrestlers' issue should not invite wider solidarity, which would have countered the strong pressure that the government was putting on the wrestlers to end their protest. It is part of its eco-system of criminalizing solidarity gestures and actions as being either motivated or anti-national.

The wrestlers withdrew their protest after the government set up a committee to inquire into their accusations. After two months of so-called inquiry, the committee, in line no doubt with what was dictated by the ministry, did a whitewash job. The role of the government was reflected in the language used by the chair of the committee, P.T. Usha, a highly respected athlete herself, who should have known better. Now a government nominated MP, she charged the wrestlers with being 'indisciplined' and 'damaging the image of India'. Thus, a protest against sexual harassment got linked with the fake nationalistic claim of defending the 'image of India' by the ruling regime.

The second time round, having learnt from their own experience of the power of solidarity and support, the wrestlers made an open appeal for support especially from women's organizations as well as political parties, which they got in ample measure. Equally importantly, there was burgeoning support from their own community in their home state of Haryana, and in neighbouring states. It was only because of the court's intervention on an appeal by the wrestlers that an FIR was filed as late as April 2023. The Delhi police, functioning directly under the jurisdiction of the central home ministry under Amit Shah, refused to take action on the FIR. On the contrary, it reiterated its brazen support for the accused on the day India's new parliament building was inaugurated amid much pomp and show. The accused MP was seen adorning one of the benches in the new parliament, applauding and cheering the prime minister's speech, while at the same time, the women wrestlers were being beaten on the streets of Delhi, forcibly removed from the protest site, cases filed against them for daring to extend their protest to a march to parliament.

The video footage of the lathi charge led to further protests forcing the government to give an assurance of taking the case forward. Subsequently, a chargesheet was framed which listed in graphic detail the blatant manner in which Singh used his power as the federation head to sexually harass, intimidate, and bully young women sportspersons into sexual contact with him. But protection for him against arrest continued. The Delhi police, in a clear case of partisanship, did not oppose his interim bail application when the matter came up in court, and so, he is free to use his position as an MP to sabotage the case and pressurize witnesses.

While the case was still in court, the government once again broke its promise of ensuring that Brij Bhushan would not be allowed to control the Wrestling Federation either directly or indirectly. This is exactly what happened when his nominees swept the so-called elections to the federation. The most insulting and demeaning remarks were made against the women wrestlers. He asserted: 'Dabdaba tha, dabdaba rahega' (my domination was there, and it will be there), after the victory of his panel. The wrestlers were distraught and demoralized. Sakshi Malik renounced her role as a wrestler; Bajrang Punia and Vinesh Phogat returned their medals. It was tragic. Not only for them, but for the fight of women for justice.

There are several conclusions which emerge from this case which throw light on the eco-system of the BJP and its government that reinforces rape cultures and impunity for the accused.

Subversion of Justice

First, the BJP and its government used their power to manipulate and subvert legal and judicial processes to save the accused. The FIR was not registered as mandated by law; there were no investigations done nor was the accused interrogated; the accused was allowed to continue in a position of power, giving him the opportunity to pressure one of the victims to withdraw her case; the chargesheet was deliberately delayed; even after the chargesheet was filed, the Delhi police did not oppose interim bail to the accused. These actions of the central government, and of the Delhi police acting at its behest, set a precedent for other cases of sexual harassment. It undermines the entire edifice of the justice system. When even in such a high-profile case an accused becomes the accuser with state patronage, it actively discourages other young women from seeking justice.

Second, the government also manipulated a so-called autonomous institution, the National Commission for Women. The NCW compromised its own mandate by maintaining a deliberate distance from the case. It took its cue not from the law, but from the ministry which is the appointing authority—the Ministry of Women and Child Welfare under Smriti Irani. Irani did not express any sympathy with the wrestlers, not a word. In June, months after the protest started, she insinuated that there was no case. She questioned why Vinesh Phogat's sister, Babita Phogat, a celebrated and accomplished wrestler herself, had not joined the struggle. It is unfortunate enough that a minister should use internal family matters in a case like this, perhaps to conceal her inability to stand for justice against her own party's Bahubali. But that this should affect the role of the NCW under her ministry shows how the subversion of autonomous institutions like the NCW, and for that matter, the National Human Rights Commission, going by their non-role in Manipur, directly impacts negatively on women's rights and the institutional support from such commissions that women are entitled to, under the law.

Third, the identity of the accused is of critical importance. If he had been a Muslim or a man from a lower caste, the female wrestlers would in all likelihood have had a better chance for justice. Brij Bhushan belongs to the powerful Thakur community, the same community as the chief minister of UP, a caste identity which helped the accused in the Hathras case escape punishment. Whereas the BJP slogan in UP is to rid politics of 'criminals', the main targets have been elected members of the minority community. Brij Bhushan is a self-declared murderer (see interview to *The Lallantop*[31]), and has many cases registered against him. Among them is an FIR registered in 1992 against 'karsevaks' under IPC Sections 147 (rioting), 153 (wantonly giving provocation with intent to cause riot), 153A (promoting enmity), 332 (voluntarily causing hurt to deter public servant from his duty), 338 (causing grievous hurt by act endangering life or personal safety of others), 295 (injuring or defiling place of worship), 297 (trespassing on burial places, etc.), 395 (dacoity) and 397 (robbery or dacoity with attempt to cause death or grievous hurt). These were recorded by him in his nomination form in 1998. Such a record, it would seem, is not a disadvantage in the BJP-RSS eco-system but a benefit.

Men like Brij Bhushan, or like the accused in the Hathras case, have the shield of impunity provided by majoritarian politics. The matter goes beyond that of a lack of political will to address crimes against women as a priority, which is common to many governments, or even the protection of their own leaders, practised by many parties in power. What we see in India today is an emerging pattern where subversion of justice commences at the very initial stage of the filing of FIRs or investigations by the police, followed by the role of the public prosecution in favouring the accused, driven not by the requirements of the law, but by the interests of the BJP agenda. The women wrestlers challenged this. Their struggle to get the serial sexual harasser arrested may not have succeeded but the struggle they fought for justice brought to light the deep challenges that all women face in accessing justice, and in fighting for the creation of an environment where women are free from fear to go about their work, their lives.

This blatant insulation from justice of one of their own, the defending of the perpetrator of sexual assault, not the victim, when the accused belongs to their ideological Parivar, has become a hallmark of the present dispensation. There are other such cases. A minister in the Haryana government, Sandeep Singh, accused of sexual harassment and charged by the police, is being protected by the government, his post secure, while the complainant, a woman sports coach in Haryana, has been suspended from her job. Earlier, in 2017, in Unnao, Uttar Pradesh, BJP MLA Kuldeep Sengar, accused of rape of a minor, was protected by the government and continued as MLA. For two years the young woman fought in every available forum. The UP government sided with the accused. The BJP protected him, refusing to demand his resignation. The girl faced extreme hardship and sorrow in her struggle for justice. In April 2018, her father was wrongly accused in a false case, beaten up by the brother of the accused MLA and jailed. He died of his injuries while in custody. After countrywide protests, the case was sent to the CBI. A year later, the young woman and her lawyer were seriously injured when a truck with its license plate blackened out hit the car she was travelling in. Clearly, there was a conspiracy to kill her and her family.

The Chief Justice of India intervened and all five cases relating to her rape and the murder of her father were transferred to Delhi courts from UP. This indicated a clear lack of trust in the impartiality of the judicial process under the UP government. On December 16, 2019, Sengar was convicted for rape. In March 2020, he was found guilty of culpable homicide and criminal conspiracy in the death of the woman's father. This is the man who was protected by the UP government. Rarely has India witnessed such an instance of struggle, courage and fortitude by a victim in the face of the repeated punishment and trauma meted out to her—to this day—for her refusal to surrender.

Sexual Harassment Against Working Women

In the case of the women wrestlers, it was found that contrary to the law—Sexual Harassment of Women at the Workplace (Prevention, Prohibition and Redressal) (PoSH) Act, 2013—there was no Internal Committee (IC) in the Wrestling Federation to inquire into cases of sexual harassment or implement the other aspects of the law. A report subsequently found that sixteen out of the thirty national sports federations had failed to set up such ICs.[32] Parliament took sixteen years to implement the Supreme Court recommendations in the landmark Vishakha judgement (1997) to enact a law against sexual harassment. But even now the law is not being implemented. The Supreme Court, while hearing the case of the women wrestlers, observed that there were 'serious lapses' in the implementation of the law and termed it a 'sorry state of affairs'. It issued several instructions, holding the Ministry of Women and Child Development responsible for getting them implemented. The ministry has yet to give a report on the implementation of the court orders. According to a survey conducted by the Indian Bar Association, 70 per cent of the respondents said they did not report sexual harassment by their superiors because they feared repercussions.[33]

Women in India have broken many barriers in their professional lives. The last two decades have seen large numbers of young women enter professional life, making a name for themselves in the media, the IT sector and service sectors apart from many other professions like nursing, the education sector and so on. Decline in opportunities in manufacturing industries have compelled poorer sections of women to seek employment as domestic workers or construction labourers. The largest number of women, according to the recent figures in the Periodic Labour Force Survey, is employed in the unorganized sector, or are self-employed. This includes mainly unpaid work in agriculture on family farms. In the unorganized sector, Adivasi women, as a community, are the highest among migrant women workers. Women's labour force participation in India is among the lowest in the world. Certainly, the main factor is the general trend of government policies which have led to the highest unemployment rates in the last two decades.

However, the issue of sexual harassment at the workplace makes the lives of working women difficult, and is one of the most underestimated issues of contemporary times. This is because of the nature of women's work. As unorganized daily workers employed through contractors and sub-contractors, with no guaranteed work conditions, they are powerless and vulnerable to sexual predators. When even in the organized sector, including in government offices and also the private sector, the legal provision for setting up internal committees to address workplace sexual harassment has not been properly implemented, one can scarcely imagine the plight of women workers in the unorganized sector.

It was a 'sathin', Bhanwari Devi's horrific experience and her fight for justice, which led to enactment of the PoSH law. Bhanwari Devi was employed in one of the flagship schemes of the Women's Development Project launched by the then Congress government in Rajasthan. She was gang raped, in September 1992, in revenge for her successful effort to prevent a child marriage, a job she was mandated to do as part of her service conditions. Bhanwari belonged to a caste lower down the caste hierarchy than her rapists, who belonged to a dominant community in the area. The police investigation was flawed and biased from the very beginning. In 1995, the court dismissed the case against the five accused on the most retrograde grounds, including that a man from a 'different' (read upper) caste cannot rape a 'lower caste woman'. This Manuvadi approach of the court was also reflected in a victory procession held by a BJP MLA of the area, one Kanhaiya Lal Meena, which was also joined by women members of the BJP. Shockingly, the appeal filed against the verdict, three decades ago, is still pending in the Rajasthan High Court.

In May 2023, the Supreme Court, hearing a case related to the PoSH Act, issued directives for its effective implementation. We do not as yet have information on the steps the government has taken to implement the court's instructions. What is apparent, however, is that the proactive steps required by governments and employers according to the law, for the prevention of sexual harassment and for encouraging working women to speak out, is non-existent. This has much to do with a social environment that puts a woman complainant of sexual harassment under scrutiny instead of the accused.

Majoritarian Weakening of the Legal Framework

One part of weakening the legal framework, as we have seen in the cases described, is the subversion of existing laws and structures. But what the BJP is doing goes far beyond, to actually add new laws which directly harm and push back against women's rights. An intrinsic aspect of a woman's equality and autonomy is the right to choose her partner. Caste entitlements find expression in barbaric practices of social violence where, if an upper-caste woman chooses to be with a man of a caste lower than hers, the dishonour brought to her family and community has to be redeemed. The methods could be decided by 'khap panchayats', the caste-based social institutions which act in such cases as a law unto themselves. Methods include boycott, eviction from homes, beatings, lynchings, and often, death.

In the second term of the UPA government, following the demands of women's movements, various court judgements and efforts of many of us who were then in parliament, a reluctant government finally agreed to draft a law to deal with crimes against women, but it was not adopted. Under the present government, even though such crimes have increased, the draft has been buried. In India, the National Family Health Surveys as well as other surveys disclose that the vast majority of couples in India, over 90 per cent, get married through 'arranged marriages' fixed by the relatives or community elders, and in urban areas, also through marriage websites. Marriages outside one's own caste account for just 5 per cent and interfaith marriages only 2 per cent. It is in this context of prevailing conservatism regarding inter-caste or interfaith marriages that governments are expected to provide support, for couples who make their own choices. But the present regime has added a dangerous new dimension to the prevailing situation in the name of 'love jihad'.

Love Jihad

The opposition to self-choice marriages has acquired a dangerous communal dimension under the BJP government with violent opposition to inter-community marriages. A Hindu girl marrying or having a relationship with a Muslim boy is termed as 'love jihad'. The theory is that Muslim men 'lure' Hindu girls into relationships, often through false identities, and then force them to convert. Numerous investigations across states, sometimes ordered by the courts, have found no such evidence either of a conspiracy or of foreign funding for such marriages. On February 4, 2020, the Union Minister of State for Home informed the parliament in a written reply that 'Article 25 of the Constitution provides for the freedom to profess, practice and propagate religion subject to public order, morality and health. The term "love jihad" is not defined under extant laws. No such case of love jihad has been reported by any of are egged on by their leaders. In a case in Bareilly, in UP, a unit of the Vishwa Hindu Parishad went into action when they heard a Hindu girl had eloped with a Muslim boy.[37] The woman was an upper-caste 27-year-old school teacher. VHP activist Sanjay Shukla, deputed to find her, is quoted as saying: 'Do your parents raise you to shame them in their old age? Why would she go with a Muslim... We have to get the woman back in our control...we have to save Hindu society.' With the help of the police, they hunted her down and brought her back within twenty-four hours. Another VHP leader, Rajesh Awasthi, is quoted as having said: 'If one daughter from our community goes to their community that means there will be ten terrorists—if she has ten children they will be terrorists.'[38] Relating one case in which he had brought the woman back, Awasthi said: 'When the girl said I will go with him [her Muslim friend] I gave her one punch and she started bleeding from the mouth. My punch is such I don't need to hit anyone a second time... I told her I will throw tezaab on you, I will cut off your nose... I will get the Muslim encountered [*sic*].'[39] Such is the violence visited on Hindu women, against their right to choice, against their autonomy and agency at the meeting point of communal and Manuvadi majoritarianism.

It is this organization, the VHP, which organized 'shaurya yatras' and campaigns, one of the purposes being to raise awareness about love jihad. They declared that participants would be trained as 'religious warriors'.[40] These are serious acts of violation of the Constitution, but who is listening? The top leaders themselves excel in hate speech. The UP chief minister said: 'I warn those who conceal their identity and play with our sisters' respect. If you don't mend your ways, your "Ram Naam Satya" [chant at Hindu funerals] journey will begin.' Sangeet Som, BJP MLA and serial offender in inciting communal violence, said: 'You must teach the love jihadis a lesson. The police and the law will take its own course and we cannot wait endlessly for this. Danda uthao ya joota (pick up a rod or a shoe) but teach them a lesson.'[41]

People like Awasthi and Som, it would appear, are above the law. They can say and do what they want, manufacture lies and destroy lives, unchecked by the law. The attacks have been taken to a higher level through collective punishment to the family of the couple, who may or may not approve of the marriage. Bulldozers destroy houses of the family of the Muslim man such as happened in Agra in UP. In Parola in Uttarakhand, a minor girl of fourteen years who went on an outing with a friend, also a Hindu, was said to have been abducted by a Muslim in a case of love jihad. Her friend took along another boy who happened to be Muslim. But the Hindutva eco-system went on a rampage, burning Muslim shops, and declaring the area to be free of Muslims. Thirty-five Muslim families, who had been living there for generations, had to flee to save their lives. The girl's uncle made a statement that since her parents had died, he was the girl's guardian and knew that this was not a case of love jihad. He appealed to the Muslims to come back. But the huge damage had been done and lives and properties destroyed.

What the poisonous 'love jihad' campaign has begun is the Ram Naam Satya of the Indian Constitution.

Love and Muslim Fundamentalism

The other side of the love jihad coin is the equally violent response of Muslim fundamentalists in cases where the girl is a Muslim and the boy a Hindu. It is true, as Nehru said, that the communalism of the majority community is more dangerous than that of the minority because it masquerades as nationalism. With the experience of almost a decade of the forces of majority communalism being in power, as we have seen, it is qualitatively worse in myriad ways, with the Constitution itself under siege.

However, the growth of Muslim fundamentalism as a counter, in the name of safeguarding the Muslim identity against the offensive of right-wing Hindutva bigots, is having a deeply negative impact on the rights and independent agency of Muslim women. For example, so-called representatives of the community, such as the Muslim Personal Law Board (MPLB), have adamantly refused to consider reform in any of the highly anti-women practices such as the arbitrary, instant triple talaq or the inhuman halala, the practice of polygamy. Many such practices do not exist in most Muslim countries, yet here in India, there is no initiative from the so-called representatives of the community for reform within the personal laws. Women's movements and specifically Muslim women's organizations have often taken the lead in campaigning for reform in Muslim personal laws. But their voices are ignored, and often, they face a backlash within their own communities.

Even after the Supreme Court verdict holding triple talaq illegal, on the plea of Muslim women, the MPLB took a most retrograde stand. The Modi government then adopted a law supposedly to help Muslim women but which in fact created fresh problems. Called the Muslim Women (Protection of Rights on Marriage) Act, 2019, it criminalized the practice of triple talaq but did not give protection to the woman. There are increasing cases of women being abandoned, of being driven out of their homes, with little legal redress. The law includes no guarantees of rights for women affected, except over their minor children, not even the right to residence. However, the MPLB castigated women going to courts instead of taking steps to protect their rights.

Where Muslim women opt to exercise their right to choose their partner, all hell breaks loose, much like in instances of caste-based honour crimes. Muslim women, caught between the aggressive majoritarian communal offensive and the utterly patriarchal and misogynist approaches of their own so-called community leaders, are in the worst position.

In the Domestic Sphere

In earlier decades, faced by the assertions and demands of women themselves, the government and parliament of the day, particularly following the Emergency, fashioned a framework of rights including laws aimed at curbing violence against women. This was done after a process of discussion and consultation with women and their organizations. In spite of weaknesses and setbacks, the laws we have in India do compare favourably with any in the world. For example, in the eighties, there was discussion on the issue of, and eventual change in, the dowry laws, on the recognition of the reality of dowry deaths to displace the false narrative of accidental 'stove bursts'. There was reform, too, in the rape laws, recognizing the critical factor of 'consent' of a woman, as opposed to examination of her past sexual history, or the practice of looking for marks on her body evidencing physical resistance, in determination of the fact of rape. In the nineties, an addition to the IPC was made for the recognition of domestic violence as a crime, taking it out of the protected 'private' sphere. A law against sex-determination was enacted after struggles waged by women against clinics which helped eliminate female foetuses; another against the practice of sati and its glorification. There was also introduced a law for the reservation of one-third of the seats for women at all levels of the panchayat and urban local bodies.

At the beginning of the twenty-first century, a civil law was enacted for the protection of women against domestic violence and of a woman's right to her home. For the first time, the law recognized and extended protection to intimate relationships outside the framework of marriage; a law was passed for the prevention of sexual harassment at the workplace for working women; amendments were made for further expansion of laws against sexual assault; specific laws for the protection of children from sexual abuse and assault were also enacted as were laws against trafficking. The last was in 2013 following nationwide protests triggered by the horrific crime known as the Nirbhaya case which took place in the national capital.

The reforms can be attributed to the courage of individual women victims, united struggles and women's organizations. The struggles took place within a secular framework. Institutions and mechanisms in defence of women's rights, such as the National Commission of Women, were also formed in this period. Special women's cells in police stations, shelters for women victims of domestic violence and help lines for urgent help were also some of the mechanisms set up.

Despite this legal framework, a combination of poor implementation, systemic patriarchy and, often, extremely regressive judicial pronouncements continued to hinder women's access to the law, reflected in the low rate of convictions for crimes against women. The specific and triple oppressions of caste, class and gender that Dalit and Adivasi women have to confront, were reflected in the official and statistical underestimation of the specific forms of violence faced by Dalit and Adivasi women. There remained many gaps in the laws.

There were social and political forces which opposed even these reforms. The struggle for advance of a rights-based framework was always in confrontation with communal and fundamentalist forces. RSS-backed women's organizations such as the Rashta Sevika Samiti, and later, the women's wing of the BJP, were not only never part of the movements, but on the contrary, opposed changes in laws to recognize domestic violence as a crime.

At the time when women were battling for the recognition of domestic violence as a crime, Mridula Sinha, then BJP Mahila Morcha president had stated on domestic violence: 'Yes, it is often the woman's fault. She can provoke a man to such an extent that he beats her... [W]e tell the woman to try and adjust...after all it is her family...'[42]

Parivar reflects the cultures being promoted which ultimately coerce women back into subordinate acceptance. When those in power hold such opinions, administrations and importantly the police also act in tandem, siding with the wife beater. The *Manusmriti* ordains: 'Though he may be bereft of virtue, given to lust and devoid of good qualities, a good woman should always worship her husband like a God.' (Chapter 5, Verse 149) Elsewhere, it states, 'As a child she must be under the protection of her father, as a wife under the protection of her husband, and when her husband is dead, by her son.'

The approaches and policies upholding the domestic role of women are a reflection of Manuvadi cultures in practice. This is of direct concern because cases of domestic abuse are steadily rising. In the latest NCRB report, 6,517 dowry deaths were registered in one year (2022). If one adds up the number of dowry deaths from 2014 to 2022, the figure is an astonishingly high number of 65,633 deaths, more than the number of soldiers killed in the wars independent India has fought. Who were these young women? By religion, almost all of them were Hindu. Who burnt them to death, or left them with no choice but to kill themselves? The men, too, were Hindu. Have you ever heard or seen a single campaign or demonstration by any organization of the Hindutva eco-system against the tradition of dowry and the violence associated with unfulfilled demands on the bride's family? They claim to be representing Hindus—but their silence when it comes to fighting such social evils as affect the women of the community is deafening. On the other hand, they laud and promote women's capacity to 'sacrifice' as an intrinsic quality of a good wife.

The eco-system of the BJP-RSS ideology never fights dowry but certainly spends a great deal of time popularizing such male-centric rituals as Karwa Chauth in states where it never existed. Recently, the prime minister has given a call to 'rich' Indians to follow the 'wed in India' policy rather than spending money on expensive destination weddings in foreign lands. The prime minister is concerned that the business should stay in India. That's fair enough. But when he thinks of weddings, has he ever thought of the bride and the expenses her family has to bear? Why is the government so unconcerned about the increase in demands for dowry and the killing of young women for dowry? It is hard to recall statements against dowry from BJP leaders. The writ of the Constitution of India guaranteeing equal citizenship does not and cannot stop at the door to the bedroom or the kitchen. Unfortunately, cultures promoted by the BJP-RSS eco-system brand such ideas as 'Western', which are therefore to be refuted as antithetical to 'our traditions'.

The attitude towards the domestic sphere being 'sacrosanct' reflects in the government's total opposition to required legal steps to protect women's bodily integrity and autonomy. In India's anti-rape laws, there was an exception to the offence of rape if the man is married and his wife is not under fifteen years of age. In other words, even if a minor of fifteen years in a child marriage did not consent to intercourse with her husband, and he had forced sex with her, it would not be considered rape. The consent of a girl was not considered necessary. Additionally, this clause was in conflict with many other laws which held the age of consent for a woman to be eighteen years. Shockingly in this case,[44] the government argued against any change in the name of a 'pragmatic view'. In its counter arguments, quite contrary to its current position on 'uniformity', the government held that 'uniformity in criteria for determining age in different context is not necessary'. It further argued that marriage 'is a bedrock of society and needs to be protected'. The Supreme Court rejected this argument of the BJP government and the anomaly of legal sanction for intercourse with a fifteen-year-old girl by her husband was removed.

The government's hypocrisy can be seen in another aspect. If a girl between the ages of 15 and 18 has consensual sex with a friend, but is not married, then that is considered rape. At least three high courts, in Delhi, Meghalaya and Karnataka, had echoed the views of women's movements when they questioned the criminalization of consensual sex between adolescents with the male partner being accused of rape, opining that the law required to be sensitized to these consensual relations between adolescents, which should be treated in a different way. But the government has refused to consider this approach.

In the ongoing case on the criminalization of marital rape in adult marriages, initially, the central government opposed it, but then sensing the inclination of courts to criminalize marital rape, took a position that it should be left to parliament to legislate and decide upon. In its petition before the Delhi High Court, the union government quoted the 'misuse of Sec 498A' to oppose criminalization of marital rape. It stated that 'gross misuse of the offence of marital rape by the wife cannot be ruled out'. The case in the Delhi High Court led to a split decision delivered in

May 2022.[45] Justice Shakhder, in favour of criminalization, noted, 'Irrespective of who the perpetrator is, forced sex mars the victim—psychologically, physically and emotionally... rape as an offence deserves societal disapprobation in the strongest terms, notwithstanding the fact that the rapist is in a marital relationship with the victim'. Justice C. Hari Shankar recorded in a dissenting note that 'Marriage between a husband and wife is not like any other relationship and the sexual aspect is the bedrock on which their marriage rests'.

The case is pending before the Supreme Court. Here too, the government has opposed criminalization. Its writ petition states: 'It would destabilize the institution of marriage apart from being an easy tool for harassing husbands'. Meanwhile, when the issue of criminalization of marital rape came up in the Rajya Sabha, it was BJP leader Sushil Modi who said 'criminalization of marital rape will end the institution of marriage'.[46] Sushil Modi's ideological predecessors like Shyama Prasad Mukherjee argued at the time of the discussions on the Hindu code bill against any rights for women in the domestic sphere, and were vociferous against the right to divorce, arguing that 'marriage is held as being sacred and sacrosanct'. All these decades later, this approach is being extended against a woman's right to bodily integrity, upholding sexual rights of a husband over his wife, even without her consent. This argument was amplified during the recent hearings on same sex marriage and the protection of the rights and against violence faced by LGBTQI+ persons.[47] The cogent reasoning advanced by the Chief Justice of India came to nought when the bench accepted the basic argument that a decision upon such a subject was outside the jurisdiction of the courts and was up to the parliament to decide.

When a country is ruled by those whose ideology is based not on the Constitution but on their selective interpretations of religion, tradition and culture, for the court to abdicate responsibility poses new challenges to those fighting for justice.

In Conclusion

Nari Shakti—Words, Deeds, Ideologies

The prime minister often speaks of nari shakti. Unlike right-wing dictators who wear their male-centric retrograde ideology on their sleeve, our prime minister is a right-wing leader with a difference. His speeches often include praise of women and their achievements. He makes it a point to seek out women achievers such as women scientists associated with the successful Chandrayaan launch and hold them up as models. All this is as it should be in any democracy. A prime minister's words encourage women and give them self-confidence. Equally, a prime minister's silence, following some of the worst atrocities committed against women, such as in the case of Bilkis Bano, or in Manipur or Hathras, demoralizes women and gives strength to the perpetrators of violence. The problem of credibility arises because the prime minister's silence is louder than his words. The chasm between slogans and practice is deep. Facts challenge the definition of 'nari shakti' as understood by the prime minister and the regime he leads. In the

Hindutva eco-system each player has their own role. The prime minister, with the shadows of words and silences, is playing his role; RSS chief Mohan Bhagwat is playing his; the BJP chief ministers adopting laws which militate against women's rights are playing their roles; the Manuvadi warriors vigilant against any sign of female assertion of sexual autonomy are playing their roles. Their common aim—to build a Hindutva rashtra.

Nari shakti is assertion, autonomy, independence; nari shakti is fighting for unity against division; nari shakti is to stand for the other, across caste and community; nari shakti is to have the strength to fight inequality, injustice. Women have been active participants in movements in defence of India's Constitution, secularism, democracy and social justice. Without these values, nari shakti can never be implemented. Moreover, in these challenging times, these issues are critical to saving the India that we love.

Acknowledgements

This is to thank the editors of Speaking Tiger, Renuka Chatterjee and Ravi Singh for their suggestion to write this essay and later their important inputs and encouragement as the work progressed. It was a pleasure to work with them. I thank Deep Narayan Chatterjee at Speaking Tiger for his editing of the manuscript.

Awstika Das, advocate, helped me with background material on the love jihad issue and particularly the various judgements. I thank her for her help.

Dr Indu Agnihotri and Dr Rajni Palriwal, my friends and comrades in decades of struggles, read the manuscript in its various stages and gave me the most useful feedback and suggestions. I am most grateful to them. I would also like to thank Pushpinder Grewal for his suggestions.

Above all I would like to thank the many victims and also families of victims of majoritarian injustice who spoke to me and particularly the family of the young woman in Hathras who was so brutally killed.

The responsibility for the mistakes or errors in this essay is entirely mine.

Notes

1 'The Prime Minister, Shri Narendra Modi addressed the nation from the ramparts of the Red Fort on the 76th Independence Day', official PMO press release (https://pib.gov.in/PressReleasePage.aspx?PRID=1852024, accessed on January 29, 2024).

2 'Union Home Ministry approved the premature release of 11 convicts in Bilkis Bano case: Gujarat Government tells Supreme Court', *The Leaflet*, October 18, 2022 (https://theleaflet.in/union-home-ministry-approved-the-premature-release-of-11-convicts-in-bilkis-bano-case-gujarat-government-tells-supreme-court/, February 19, 2022.)

3 *Organiser*, November 30, 1949.

4 Chapter 1, page 73, *Manusmriti* (Delhi: Arsh Sahitya Prachar Trust, 2005).

5 'Kids' "private parts" lesson: RSS chief blames "leftist attack", cites Trump example', *India Today*, September 18, 2023 (https://www.indiatoday.in/india/story/kids-private-parts-names-leftist-attack-gone-too-far-rss-chief-mohan-bhagwat-2437013-2023-09-18, accessed on January 29, 2024).

6 Vinayak Damodar Savarkar, *Six Glorious Epochs of Indian History*, translated and edited by S.T. Godbole, (Bombay: Bal Savarkar, 1971).

7 'Bilkis Bano: "I Want Justice, Not Revenge, I Want My Daughters to Grow Up in a Safe India"', *The Wire*, May 9, 2017 (https://thewire.in/law/i-want-justice-not-revenge-bilkis-

bano-expresses-gratitude-to-mumbai-high-court, accessed on January 29, 2024).

8 'Bilkis Bano case convicts' release: Two had open "outraging woman's modesty case", one missed parole', *Deecan Herald*, October 19, 2022 (https://www.deccanherald.com/india/bilkis-bano-case-convicts-release-two-had-open-outraging-woman-s-modesty-case-one-missed-parole-1155144.html, accessed on January 29, 2024).

9 'Centre cleared release of Bilkis case convicts, CBI & court opposed: Gujarat', *The Indian Express*, October 17, 2022 (https://indianexpress.com/article/india/bilkis-bano-case-govt-approves-premature-release-of-11-life-term-convicts-gujarat-8214503/, accessed on January 29, 2024).

10 'Now, BJP MLA says Bilkis Bano's rapists "are Brahmins with good sanskaar"', *Hindustan Times*, August 18, 2022 (https://www.hindustantimes.com/india-news/now-bjp-mla-says-bilkis-bano-s-rapists-are-brahmins-with-good-sanskaar-101660835567829.html, accessed on January 30, 2024).

11 'Delhi gang rape verdict: By invoking "collective conscience", the Supreme Court sidestepped justice', *Scroll.in*, May 13, 2017 (https://scroll.in/article/837215/delhi-gang-rape-verdict-by-invoking-collective-conscience-the-supreme-court-sidestepped-justice, accessed on January 29, 2024).

12 'Manipur Mob on Rescue Mission', *The Telegraph*, September 9, 2023 (https://epaper.telegraphindia.com/calcutta/2023-09-09/71/Page-1.html, accessed on January 29, 2024).

13 *Organiser*, 21 May 2023.

14 '17 years since their naked protest against Army, "Mothers of Manipur" say fight not over yet', *The Print*, July 22, 2021 (https://theprint.in/india/17-years-since-their-naked-protest-against-army-mothers-of-manipur-say-fight-not-over-yet/700093/, accessed on January 29, 2024).

15 Protection of Children from Sexual Offences (POCSO) Act,

2012 was amended in 2019 to raise the minimum punishment for penetrative assault from 7 to 10 years, and to 20 years if the victim is below 16 years of age, with a maximum punishment of life imprisonment and a provision for the death penalty in cases of aggravated penetrative assault.

16 'Harassment of Indian Muslim women on apps must be prosecuted, says UN official', *Scroll.in*, January 12, 2022 (https://scroll.in/latest/1014893/harassment-of-indian-muslim-women-on-apps-must-be-condemned-prosecuted-says-un-official, accessed on January 30, 2024).

17 'They will enter your houses, rape sisters and daughters: BJP's Parvesh Verma on Shaheen Bagh protesters', *INDIA TV*, January 28, 2020 (https://www.indiatvnews.com/news/india/bjp-mp-parvesh-verma-shaheen-bagh-protesters-583674, accessed on January 30, 2024).

18 'Assam CM Himanta Biswa Sarma gives hate speeches in poll bound Karnataka, indulges in a divisive diatribe', *Citizens for Justice and Peace*, March 16, 2023 (https://cjp.org.in/assam-cm-himanta-biswa-sarma-gives-hate-speeches-in-poll-bound-karnataka-indulges-in-a-divisive-diatribe/, accessed on January 30, 2024).

19 Vinayak Damodar Savarkar, *Essentials of Hinduism* (Hindi Sahitya Sadan, 1923).

20 V.D. Savarkar, see Note 6.

21 'Hindu society has been at war for over 1000 years. It is natural for people those at war to be aggressive', *Organiser*, January 10, 2023 (https://organiser.org/2023/01/10/ 104033/rss-news/hindu-society-has-been-at-war-for-over-1000-years-it-is-natural-for-people-those-at-war-to-be-aggressive/#google_vignette, accessed on January 31, 2024).

22 'Keep your knives sharpened at home, says BJP MP Pragya Thakur at Hindu convention', *The Indian Express*, December 26, 2022 (https://indianexpress.com/article/political-pulse/keep-knives-sharpened-bjp-mp-pragya-thakur-love-jihad-shivamogga-8345187/, accessed on January 31, 2024).

23 'BJP Mahila Morcha Leader Says Hindus Should Gangrape Muslim Women; Gets Expelled', *The Wire*, June 30, 2019 (https://thewire.in/communalism/bjp-mahila-morcha-leader-says-hindus-should-gangrape-muslim-women-gets-expelled, accessed on January 31, 2024).

24 'Sadhvi Vibhanand's Call to "Rape" Muslim Women With Impunity Shows Hindutva's Politics of Fear', *The Wire*, February 12, 2022 (https://thewire.in/communalism/sadhvi-vibhanands-call-to-rape-muslim-women-with-impunity-shows-hindutvas-politics-of-fear, accessed on January 31, 2024).

25 'Rapes happen in India, not Bharat: RSS chief Mohan Bhagwat blames western culture for gangrapes', *India Today*, January 4, 2013 (https://www.indiatoday.in/india/story/rapes-happen-in-india-not-bharat-rss-chief-mohan-bhagwat-blames-western-culture-for-gangrapes- 150752-2013-01-03, accessed on January 29, 2024).

26 'Women crossing Laxman-rekha will be punished: BJP leader', *Firstpost.com*, January 4, 2013 (https://www.firstpost.com/politics/women-who-cross-laxman-rekha-will-be-punished-bjp-leader-578003.html, accessed on January 29, 2024).

27 'UP Anti-Romeo squads arrested 14,454 people since 2017, police say in RTI reply', *India Today*, January 13, 2023 (https://www.indiatoday.in/india/story/up-anti-romeo-squads-arrested-people-police-rti-reply-1758791- 2021-01-13, accessed on February 7, 2024).

28 'Such women are always found dead in millet fields: BJP leader's shocking remark on Hathras victim', *India Today*, October 7, 2020 (https://www.indiatoday.in/india/story/such-women-are-always-found-dead-in-millet-fields-bjp-leader-s-shocking-remark-on-hathras-victim-1729065-2020-10-06, accessed on January 29, 2024).

29 '"Rape Cases Can Be Stopped Only With *Sanskar* Not Governance": UP BJP MLA', *NDTV.com*, October 4, 2020 (https://www.ndtv.com/india-news/bjp-mla-surendra-

singh-says-rape-cases-can-be-stopped-only-with-sanskar-not-governance-2304834, accessed on January 29, 2024).

30 Godavari Parulekar, *Adivasis Revolt: The Story of Warli Peasants in Struggle* (Calcutta: National Book Agency, 1975).

31 BJP MP Brij Bhushan Singh Interview to Saurabh Tripathi, *The Lallantop*, YouTube, February 21, 2022 (https://www.youtube.com/watch?v=HFy1NWAq8C4, accessed on January 29, 2024).

32 'Not just wrestling, half of national sports federations don't have sexual harassment panel mandated by law', *The Indian Express*, May 4, 2023 (https://indianexpress.com/article/sports/not-just-wrestling-half-of-national-sports-federations-dont-have-sexual-harassment-panel-mandated-by-law-8590204/, accessed on January 30, 2024).

33 'Most women still don't report sexual harassment at work: Study', *Hindustan Times*, January 4, 2017 (https://www.hindustantimes.com/delhi/most-women-still-don-t-report-sexual-harassment-at-work-study/story-8Efvy12aScvKBsAkoAxy2I.html, accessed on January 30, 2024).

34 Government of India, Ministry of Home Affairs, February 4, 2020. Available online: https://www.mha.gov.in/MHA1/Par2017/pdfs/par2020-pdfs/ls-04022020/23.pdf, accessed on January 31, 2024.

35 'Lies, Insistence and Disregard for Evidence: The Journey of "Love Jihad" Laws', *The Wire*, December 30, 2022 (https://thewire.in/communalism/lies-insistence-and-disregard-for-evidence-the-journey-of-love-jihad-laws, accessed on January 30, 2024).

36 'Kanpur "Love Jihad" SIT Finds No Funding or Organised Conspiracy', *The Quint*, November 23, 2020 (https://www.thequint.com/news/india/kanpur-sit-love-jihad-report-no-funding-organised-conspiracy-seen, accessed on January 30, 2024).

37 'Hindu Vigilantes Work With Police to Enforce "Love Jihad"

Law In North India', *The Intercept*, July 3, 2021 (https://theintercept.com/2021/07/03/love-jihad-law-india/, accessed on January 30, 2024).

38 Ibid.

39 Ibid.

40 'Will the multiple upcoming yatras by VHP & affiliates remain peaceful?', *Citizens for Justice and Peace*, September 30, 2023 (https://cjp.org.in/will-the-multiple-upcoming-yatras-by-vhp-affiliates-remain-peaceful/, accessed on January 30, 2024).

41 'Must teach the love-jihadis a lesson: BJP MLA Sangeet Som asks youth to pursue tit-for-tat policy', Bangalore Mirror, November 3, 2020 (https://bangaloremirror.indiatimes.com/news/india/must-teach-the-love-jihadis-a-lesson-bjp-mla-sangeet-som-asks-youth-to-pursue-tit-for-tat-policy/articleshow/79020038.cms, accessed on January 31, 2024).

42 'BJP's Attitude to Women', *Sabrang.com*, September 1, 1999 (https://www.sabrang.com/prelease/ealert/elec8.htm, accessed on January 30, 2024).

43 'RSS chief Mohan Bhagwat at it again, says women should be just housewives and husbands should be the breadwinners', *India Today*, January 6, 2013 (https://www.indiatoday.in/india/north/story/rss-mohan-bhagwat-at-it-again-says-women-should-be-just-housewives-and-husbands-should-be-the-breadwinners-150908-2013-01-05, accessed on January 30, 2024).

44 *Independent Thought vs Union of India & Anr* (WP [Civil] 382 of 2013).

45 Delhi High Court in *Farhan vs State & Anr*, on May 11, 2022 (https://indiankanoon.org/doc/124655100/, accessed on January 30, 2024).

46 'Criminalisation of marital rape will end institution of marriage: BJP MP Shushil Modi', *The Meghalayan*, February 2, 2022 (https://themeghalayan.com/criminalisation-of-marital-rape-will-end-institution-of-marriage-bjp-mp-shushil-modi/, accessed on January 30, 2024).

47 Supreme Court of India in *Supriyo @ Supriya Chakraborty & Anr vs Union of India*, on October 17, 2023 (https://indiankanoon.org/doc/129202312/, accessed on January 30, 2024).

ALSO IN SPEAKING TIGER

DISGRACE

Global Reflections on Sexual Violence

Joanna Bourke

> '[A] monumental feat of research and an act of political scrutiny at its most far-reaching. From India to Haiti, from Abu Ghraib to Namibia, Bourke trails the cruel incidence of rape across the globe.... *Disgrace* will become required reading for anyone seeking to put rape at the forefront of the struggle to make the world a better and safer place.'
>
> —Jacqueline Rose, author of *On Violence Against Women*

This unprecedented study of rape culture explores how sexual violence varies widely across time and place, from nineteenth-century peasant women in Ireland who were abducted as a way of forcing marriage, to date-raped high-school students in twentieth-century America; and from girls and women violated by Russian soldiers in 1945, to Dalit women raped by men of higher castes today. The book delves into the factors that facilitate violence—including institutions, ideologies, and practices—but also gives voice to survivors and activists, drawing inspiration from their struggles. Ultimately, Joanna Bourke intends to forge a transnational feminism that will promote a more harmonious, equal and rape- and violence-free world.

ALSO IN SPEAKING TIGER

THE FREE VOICE

On Democracy, Culture and the Nation

Ravish Kumar

The best-selling, landmark collection by one of India's bravest journalists, re-issued with new essays on the state of India's democracy and media ahead of the 2024 general election.

Ravish Kumar is perhaps India's most forthright, principled and courageous journalist. He is also one of our most insightful social and political commentators. *The Free Voice* was first published in 2018 and has been read by several thousand readers in both English and Hindi for the clarity with which it examines the Indian political, social and cultural landscape—the climate of fear created by a majoritarian and authoritarian government since 2014; the failure of institutions meant to safeguard the country's democracy; violence against minority groups and dissenters; threats to free expression; crony capitalism and the near-complete transformation of the media into an instrument of propaganda. In this revised edition have been added new essays on the state of the nation that Ravish wrote after he resigned from NDTV when it was taken over by the controversial Adani Group.

'This brave and timely book should be required reading for every Indian.'

—Nayantara Sahgal